The Future of the Humanities

Walter
Kaufmann

with a new introduction
by Saul Goldwasser

The Future
of the
Humanities

Teaching Art, Religion,
Philosophy, Literature,
and History

Transaction Publishers
New Brunswick (U.S.A) and London (U.K.)

New material this edition copyright © 1995 by Transaction Publishers, New Brunswick, New Jersey 08903. Originally published in 1977 by Reader's Digest Press.

This book is printed on acid-free paper that meets the American National Standard for Permanence of Paper for Printed Library Materials.

Library of Congress Catalog Number: 94-31501
ISBN: 1-56000-780-X
Printed in the United States of America

Library of Congress Cataloging-in-Publication Data

Kaufmann, Walter Arnold.
    The future of the humanities : teaching art, religion, philosophy, literature, and history / Walter Kaufmann ; with a new introduction by Saul Goldwasser.
        p. cm. — (Foundations of higher education)
    Originally published: New York : Reader's Digest Press, 1977.
    Includes bibliographical references and index.
    ISBN 1-56000-780-X
    1. Humanities—Study and teaching (Higher)—United States.   I. Title.
II. Series.
AZ183.U5K38   1994
001.3—dc20   94-31501
                                                                              CIP

Transaction Books by Walter Kaufmann

Freud, Adler, and Jung,
with a new introduction by Ivan Soll

The Future of the Humanities,
with a new introduction by Saul Goldwasser

Goethe, Kant, and Hegel,
with a new introduction by Ivan Soll

Nietzsche, Heidegger, and Buber,
with a new introduction by Ivan Soll

Religion from Tolstoy to Camus,
with a new introduction by Paul Gottfried

I dedicate this book to those
from whom I acquired
   my first love
of the humanities

     MY PARENTS

     AND

     MY MOTHER'S FATHER

CONTENTS

INTRODUCTION TO THE TRANSACTION EDITION

Walter Kaufmann's analysis of the humanities came near the end of a lifetime that, in a sense, reflected what the humanities are all about. He was, at once, both a contributor and an acute observer of the *studia humanitatis* and more.

It has been almost two decades since the original publication of *The Future of the Humanities*. The opening line of the Prologue still rings true today: "The humanities are adrift." What has changed is that not only are the humanities adrift, but they are under attack. We are now greeted with the attempt to redefine our cultural heritage and, utilizing the ambiguous concept multiculturalism, the acceptable canon under which such a change can be accomplished.

The Humanities and Humanity

Professor Kaufmann, writing in an erudite but accessible style, addresses many of the key issues within the humanities that still persist today. The main character in Moliere's *Le Bourgeois Gentilhomme* suddenly discovers that he has been speaking prose all his life. From the start of his career, Kaufmann had been addressing human issues, but he was consciously aware of what needed to be done in order to affirm and retain our humanity.

If the educative process is to be successful, it is incumbent upon professors to induce, and students to experience, culture shock. Culture shock results from examining alternatives, and from alternatives emerge possible varieties of *Weltanschauungen*. The achievement of alternative views is a central theme of this work. Kaufmann was at home in many parts of the world and immersed himself in the life of the indigenous population of the countries in which he traveled, whether it was Mexico or the Middle East, India or Thailand, Japan or Fiji. He admonishes the American traveler to stay out of Hiltons with their familiar and comfortable accommodations. Much before his time, Kaufmann celebrated multiculturalism in what is perhaps the truer sense of the term.

Kaufmann makes clear that his aim is not to predict what the future of the humanities will be but to influence them. One way to influence them is to offer a diagnosis of what he believed went wrong and to suggest how they should be taught. He notes that "what is at stake is nothing less than the future of humanity," and, further on, that "it is widely felt that the humanities may hold the key to the future of humanity." Kaufmann does not feel the need to argue this point; rather it is assumed. While this connection may be too simple and in itself not sufficient, a good argument can be made that it is a necessary one. If the study of the humanities does have the power to transform us, as was originally thought to be the case in fifteenth-century Renaissance Italy, and inculcate a moral transformation within our innermost being, then humanistic inquiry is an essential enterprise.[1]

Defining the Humanities

Defining the humanities is not without some controversy. Kaufmann locates the humanities in six general fields of study: religion and philosophy, art and music, and literature and history. Literature could be studied within a language or within a variety of languages in language departments. The National Endowment for the Humanities further includes linguistics, jurisprudence, archeology, and "those aspects of the social sciences which have humanistic content and employ humanistic methods." Precisely what the content and methods referred to are, is not defined.[2]

While Kaufmann, in his delineation of the humanities in the Prologue, does not mention some of the areas that have in more recent time been included along with the traditional *studia humanitatis,* he does utilize these added areas of study. In the last chapter he proposes, by way of a paradigmatic interdisciplinary course, a whole semester's study around some selected problem areas. One of the areas that he was not unfamiliar with was the area of punishment.[3] Using punishment as one of his examples, he notes that there are a variety of disciplines from which the area has been studied besides philosophy and religion. Punishment has also been studied "in courses on Greek tragedy taught in the department of classics, in courses on Russian novels, in political theory, psychology, sociology and anthropology, as well as law schools." In the course that Kaufmann proposes as an exemplar, "students would read relevant literature in all the fields mentioned and listen to professors from different disciplines."

I will have more to say about Kaufmann's position on interdisciplinary approaches to the humanities a bit further on.

Suffice for now to note that Kaufmann eschews the attempt to compress the humanities into autonomous departmentalized areas with artificial and arbitrary boundaries. There is always a larger context in which to examine a particular philosopher or artist, a particular text or artistic creation.

Given Kaufmann's view on what the humanities entail, it is somewhat puzzling to peruse some of the reviews that greeted *The Future of the Humanities* when it first appeared. There are misinterpretations about what the book purports to do even though it is clearly stated at the outset that its "aim is not to predict but to influence" the future of the humanities. Kaufmann is also accused of being a "donnish" Princeton professor. Here was one reviewer who apparently did not conquer, or care to read, the chapter "The Art of Reading" or carefully read the one entitled "Translating and Editing" where Kaufmann calls reviewers to account. One need only examine Kaufmann's proposed course on punishment. He would have students attend trials, teach in the prisons whenever possible, and have some concrete interactive experience with prisoners. It can hardly be the case that donnishness and coming to grips with the criminal justice system go hand-in-hand.[4]

In an otherwise extraordinary work,[5] Robert Proctor limits the humanities to what they were for Petrarch and his followers, the focus being a return to the study of Greek and Roman languages and literature, and to classical antiquity in general. He states that "there can thus be no such thing as a 'modern humanism' divorced from what the humanities originally were: the study of the Greeks and the Romans as models for individual and collective behavior."[6] The Renaissance humanists turned to the ancients in order to revitalize and perfect their own center of being. However, it is paradoxical that the ancients to whom they turned had a notion of the self that affirmed itself by losing itself as it became identified with the larger cosmos, the Logos. The metaphysical assumptions that such a position presupposes will simply not stand up to contemporary philosophical scrutiny. In spite of this, Proctor believes that if we desire identification with the tradition of the humanities, we must study the Greeks and Romans, just as religious individuals must study their respective religious traditions. Further, while Dante, Shakespeare, or Tolstoy may be rewarding to study, such an endeavor can "create only confusion, and make it difficult to understand and use our cultural inheritance, when we include those writers under the rubric 'humanities.' They belong to other traditions."[7] Proctor's position is simply too narrowly conceived.

That Kaufmann's conception of the humanities is much wider than Proctor's needs little confirmation. At first it might indeed seem strange that the author of *Faith of a Heretic* and author and translator of so much of Nietzsche should emphasize religion to the extent that he does. Yet if one were to examine Kaufmann's published works, one could not help but be struck by the number of works on religion: *Religion From Tolstoy to Camus*,[8] *Critique of Religion and Philosophy*,[9] *Religions in Four Dimensions, Existentialism, Religion and Death*,[10] and *Judaism and Christianity: Essays by Leo Baeck*.[11] In *Religions in Four Dimensions*, published one year before *The Future of the Humanities*, Kaufmann, never short of hyperbole, asserts that "there is no subject more important than religion. It involves the most fateful questions.... I feel that those who close their eyes to the great religions are thoughtless, and, in effect, refuse to think about alternative answers to some of the most crucial questions."[12] A similar statement appears in Section 45 of this work where Kaufmann argues that "there can hardly be a more important subject than *comparative religion*."

One caveat is necessary should one think Kaufmann is affirming a religious perspective: it is that such a subject should not be taught by an apologist, and that it should, instead, ulti-

mately provide students with alternative views so that critical scrutiny can lead to growth. It is in comparative religions
and scripture that "Socratic teachers and dialectical readers
can scarcely hope to find materials that are worthier of their
best efforts and more appropriate for humanistic education."
In his introduction to Kaufmann's *Discovering the Mind,* Ivan
Soll points out that Nietzsche's influence on Kaufmann re-
flects a style that displays a rapid development of ideas without being bogged down in minutia that could impede the
intended goal. Thus, there is a "deliberate decision not to attempt to offer an overly full account of the material in which
his major thesis and insights would lose a great deal of their
force in a sea of related but not directly relevant detail."[13] No
doubt what underlies this approach is Kaufmann's contempt
for those who display the turn of mind he calls scholastic. It
is the kind of mind that is irredeemably microscopic. The
question is how to determine which works one ought to accept into the body of humanistic inquiry. Kaufmann, in *The
Future of the Humanities,* is suggestive of which works and
which creative individuals to include, even going so far as to
offer a list. At other times he makes polemical pronouncements, such as the status he gives the modern German artist,
Käthe Kollwitz, which is sure to raise exception. Nevertheless, a fuller determination of where Kaufmann stands in regard to what should be included or excluded within the
enterprise of humanistic study can, in part, be achieved by
focusing on the greater body of his works. The chapter in this
work that discusses how to read, particularly dialectical reading, is germane to this determination. The third element—
dialectical reading that includes the historical-philosophical
element—is applicable here.

In the conclusion of *The Future of the Humanities* Kaufmann
states that what he presents "is not a blueprint for a new academy. It is a call for serious reflection." Nothing is cast in stone.

Yet it is safe to say that any debate about what constitutes the heart of the humanities must be determined within the academy itself, where, even there, there are still no guarantees of consensus. Roger Shattuck argues that this debate as to the choice of inclusion should be not only among teachers and professors but also among "a few branch committees," "the federal government," "school districts," and "publishers."[14] That would be a most dangerous thing to do. Whether one is determining the canon of the social sciences or the humanities, "when it is mandated by external interest groups, the potential for dogma and doctrine grows exponentially."[15]

Approaching the Humanities:
Kinds of Minds and Reading

Kaufmann's analysis of the four kinds of minds as they are found within academia and reading as the heart of the humanities should be a necessary prolegomenon to every undergraduate and graduate student on college campuses. One might hasten to include even beginning instructors. Thirty years of teaching and lecturing at a number of universities, nationally and internationally, provide us with insights from an observer whose polemical account is witty but probing, acerbic but critically constructive and, above all, honest.[16]

There are two points to keep in mind when reading Kaufmann. The first is that, as Ivan Soll notes, Kaufmann's writings are always infused with passion and personal preferences that are unusual to find in an academic setting.[17] Some reviewers of Kaufmann's work simply do not know what to make of this. They prefer a style of writing that is bloodless and neutered. If there was not a critical and historical consciousness behind his analysis, then perhaps their criticisms would seem justified. But that is not the case.

A second point to keep before the reader is that while Kaufmann would be the last person to maintain that ideas and theories cannot be examined in themselves, he also believes that they must be examined in their wider existential context. Again, this is a break from conventional academic writing and, on the surface, can appear to be *ad hominem*. However, as Professor Soll notes, if this were the only way to understand the products of human creation, then the charge of reductionism could be justified.[18] Instead, Kaufmann offers reasoned arguments, examples, and theoretical frameworks from which to understand and enhance our knowledge of the object of inquiry. Each philosopher, literary figure, scientist, or artist is examined within a cultural context. That context is only one aspect among others that commands our attention. In *The Future of the Humanities,* Kaufmann argues that if one wishes to determine the adequacy of an interpretive judgment, it may be necessary to understand the "author's *geistige Persönlichkeit*—his cast of mind, or in one word, his mentality." What is called for is an examination of the whole person within an existential context.

There are four categories of professors: visionaries, scholastics, Socratics, and journalists. Implied but not explicitly stated is the fact that each type influences their students according to a pedagogical style that effects its content. The current dominant form, the scholastic type, has had a particularly pernicious effect on graduate education and also in the direction that academia has taken.

The positive characteristics of a scholastic professor include the rigor with which he approaches his subject, a well-formed specialization, and a sense of professionalism. However, for Kaufmann, the negative characteristics far outweigh the positive ones: allegiance to consensus, microscopic vision, and an inordinate degree of misconception of subject matter. This is a major factor effecting the unfortunate direction that humanities education has taken.[19]

There are at least two reasons for this egregious turn in direction. The first is that since the end of World War II, the influx of students and the expansion of colleges necessitated a rapid increase in faculty. Kaufmann states that "in the process academia became infinitely more professional, scholastic, and anti-socratic." Quantities of students compel quantitative testing. Professionalism compels the quantitative production of publications.

A second reason for a scholastic turn was the result of humanities professors emulating their colleagues in the sciences. Such genuflection, modeled not on great scientists but on scientific scholastics, could eventuate in monetary rewards, leaves, and promotions. In *The Genealogy of Morals,* Nietzsche indicts both science and scholars: "The proficiency of our finest scholars, their heedless industry, their heads smoking day and night, their very craftsmanship—how often the real meaning of all this lies in the desire to keep something hidden from oneself! Science as a means of self-narcosis: *do you have an experience of that?*"[20] A bit further on, Nietzsche states that what is feared most is "*regaining consciousness.*" There are still attempts to model the humanities on the sciences. For Kaufmann, this is a disastrous course to pursue.[21]

The Socratic type of mind is the perfect antidote for scholasticism. Rigorous examination is retained, but included is a confrontation with consensus, faith, morals, and ideologies. The Socratic approach applies to all the humanities and, Kaufmann specifically notes, to "politics and economics, sociology and anthropology." Kaufmann is well aware of what can happen when professionalism dominates and where professors do not have the moral rectitude to question the moral and political climate of the state. Who, he asks, is in a better position to do this? And who is in a better position to inculcate the necessary critical attitude that students need? Both faculty and students in Nazi Germany were quick to side with National Socialism. Any philosophical stance is always viewed in a wider context of alternatives. One reason, among many, that Kaufmann was particularly critical of Heidegger was because of his political myopia and his embrace of Nazism.[22]

Kaufmann has the greatest contempt for journalistic type professors—they teach what is *au courant,* but like yesterday's headlines, the content of such inquiry is quickly forgotten and justifiably so.[23] The courses offered under this category deflect energy that could best be spent examining some of the world's great works. The fourth type of mind is the visionary. One wonders how often they appear on college campuses. Nietzsche and Wittgenstein did appear for a brief while, but visionaries are loners who are too provocative. They are the least likely to conform to accepted norms, particularly in academia. Worse, they do not necessarily make the best teachers. Kaufmann's analysis of this phenomenon is enlightening. Nevertheless, from a humanistic point of view, we need them: the contributions they make are incalculable. Recognizing that vision is an extraordinary gift, Kaufmann is bold enough to offer us a chapter on whether such a talent can be taught.

Reading, editing, translating, and reviewing can be viewed as parts of a seamless whole. Kaufmann was a gifted translator and scholar, and because he was both, he knew how important it is to be able to read well. The special demands of translating, whether it was Goethe's *Faust,* Nietzsche's *Thus Spoke Zarathustra,* or Buber's *I and Thou,* required a certain sensitivity, comprehension, and creative talent if it was to be done well. Kaufmann believes that being able to read well is absolutely crucial for students: "Reading is the core of the humanities and of the social sciences, but most students never learn to read well."

It may not be only students who do not read well. One of Kaufmann's central criticisms of Heidegger is that he is an exegetical reader (along with Kierkegaard and Sartre) and as a result, he did not read Nietzsche well. The kind of reading that Kaufmann wishes to teach is dialectical, which borrows from Socrates, Hegel, and Buber, and is brought together in an original synthesis. The *sine quo non* of dialectical reading is culture shock. Dialectical readers subject themselves to multiple shocks while exegetical readers shun them. Life, faith, and values must be open to critical scrutiny and alternative possibilities.

Religion and the Interdisciplinary Approach

Religion, particularly comparative religion, acts as a focal point from which students can "examine their own faith and morals and the ideologies and values of their parents, peer groups, and society." This theme had been developed in earlier works but became forcefully presented in *Religions in Four Dimensions,* where Kaufmann states that "there is no subject more important than religion. It involves the most fateful questions, to which different religions give different answers."[24] In *The Future of the Humanities,* the point is made that religious texts provide the perfect subject matter for Socratic scrutiny and dialectical reading. It provides students with alternative choices, with culture shock.

Professor Kaufmann was not only an acknowledged scholar in German philosophy, Nietzsche in particular, but also a translator and editor of philosophers, poets, and theologians. He published his own poetry and was a photographer of some renown.[25] Kaufmann's reputation needs no enhancement. It is important to make note of this so that it is understood that it is one thing for someone to say that this is what must be done. It is quite another thing to say something and actually do it. In *Religions in Four Dimensions* Kaufmann states that "my primary concern throughout is existential. I mean that it is not with beliefs and speculations, with theology and metaphysics, but with humanity. And I feel strongly that without this dimension even a good historical and comparative study would lack depth."[26]

Photography, for Kaufmann, was an alternative way of seeing, the way that philosophy and scholarship are ways of seeing. Photography, like the other creative arts, becomes a metaphor for vision. It needs utilization particularly when philosophy and scholarship become training grounds in microscopy and a preparation for blindness. *Religions in Four Dimensions* is itself an example of an interdisciplinary approach. Kaufmann reaches a culminating point in his long career when he states that "I have come to believe that the most important thing a scholar or a poet can hope to try to teach is vision, or to put the point more modestly, to see better."[27]

An interdisciplinary approach does not preclude rigor. That characteristic of the scholastic mind is an essential basis for visionary development and critical scrutiny of social consensus and values. Becoming an interdisciplinarian requires a firm grasp of one discipline and the courage to move into another discipline along with the possibility of concomitant innovation.[28]

In the last chapter of *The Future of the Humanities*, Kaufmann states that "a departmental approach is always abstract." A subject area can become artificially constricted, and isolated characteristics can become the object of inquiry. Kaufmann offers suggestions for interdisciplinary work around topics such as punishment, and death and dying. Kaufmann had previously done work in these areas. Two works, *Existentialism, Religion and Death* and *Man's Lot: A Trilogy*[29] are cases in point. *Man's Lot*, like *Religions in Four Dimensions,* is interspersed with photographs, a scholarly text, and poetry. The book concludes with a striking photograph

(1977) of the cemetery inside the Capuchin church on the Via Veneto, Rome, where rows of skulls and a skeletal figure in a monk's robe confront the reader.

Concluding Remarks

Some years ago, I taught an honors course entitled "Methods in Religion and Philosophy." Part of the text included Kaufmann's *The Faith of a Heretic*. One day I received a note from one of my students indicating how moved she was by a particular passage from the chapter entitled "Death," near the end of that book. I still have the note. Of all his writings, it is my favorite passage too. It was also read at a memorial service for Kaufmann on the Princeton University campus in December 1980. I believe the passage is an appropriate introduction to *The Future of the Humanities*.

> The Greeks had considered hope the final evil in Pandora's box. They also gave us an image of perfect nobility: a human being lovingly doing her duty to another human being despite all threats, and going to her death with pride and courage, not deterred by any hope—Antigone.
>
> Hopelessness is despair. Yet life without hope is worth living. As Sartre's Orestes says: "Life begins on the other side of despair." But is hope perhaps resumed on the other side? It need not be. In honesty, what is there to hope for? Small hopes remain but do not truly matter. I may hope that the sunset will be clear, that the night will be cool and still, that my work will turn out well, and yet know that nine hopes out of ten are not even remembered a year later. How many are recalled a century hence? A billion years hence?

> The cloud-capp'd towers, the gorgeous palaces,
> The solemn temples, the great globe itself,
> Yea, all which it inherit, shall dissolve;
> And, like this insubstantial pageant faded,
> Leave not a rack behind. We are such stuff

As dreams are made on, and our little life
Is rounded with a sleep.

(The Tempest, IV, i)

It is possible that this is wrong. There may be surprises in store for us, however improbable it seems and however little evidence suggests it. But I do not hope for that. Let people who do not know what to do with themselves in this life, but fritter away their time reading magazines and watching television, hope for eternal life. If one lives intensely, the time comes when sleep seems bliss. If one loves intensely, the time comes when death seems bliss.

Those who loved with all their heart and mind and might have always thought of death, and those who knew the endless nights of harrowing concern for others have longed for it.

The life I want is a life I could not endure in eternity. It is a life of love and intensity, suffering and creation, that makes life worth while and death welcome. There is no other life I should prefer. Neither should I like not to die.

If I ask myself who in history I might like to have been, I find that all the men I most admire were by most standards deeply unhappy. They knew despair. But their lives were worth while—I only wish mine equaled theirs in this respect—and I have no doubt that they were glad to die.

As one deserves a good night's sleep, one also deserves to die. Why should I hope to wake again? To do what I have not done in the time I've had? All of us have so much more time than we use well. How many hours in a life are spent in a way of which one might be proud, looking back?

For most of us death does not come soon enough. Lives are spoiled and made rotten by the sense that death is distant and irrelevant. One lives better when one expects to die, say, at forty, when one says to oneself long before one is twenty: whatever I may be able to accomplish, I should be able to do by then; and what I have not done by then, I am not likely to do ever. One cannot count on living until one is forty—or thirty—but it makes for a better life if one has a rendezvous with death.

Not only love can be deepened and made more intense and impassioned by the expectation of impending death; all of life is enriched by it. Why deceive myself to the last moment, and hungrily devour sights, sounds, and smells only when it is almost too late? In our treatment of others, too, it is well to remember that they will die: it makes for greater humanity.[30]

Notes

1. Gregory Vlastos comes close to arguing a similar point in "Graduate Education in the Humanities: Reflections and Proposals," in *The Philosophy and Future of Graduate Education,* ed. William Frankena (Ann Arbor: The University of Michigan Press, 1980), 66.
2. For an exemplary classification of the humanities, see William G. Bowen and Julie Ann Sosa, *Prospects for Faculty in the Arts and Sciences* (Princeton: Princeton University Press, 1989), 189–90.
3. See Walter Kaufmann, *Without Guilt and Justice* (New York: Peter H. Wyden, Inc., 1973). In 1971, I invited Kaufmann to meet with a group of my ethics students at the Trenton State Prison while we were studying Nietzsche's *Thus Spoke Zarathustra.* After nearly three hours of an exhausting meeting with the student-inmates, I had to call an end because of the conclusion of visiting hours. I believe Kaufmann could have continued for several hours more.
4. In *Faith of a Heretic* (New York: Meridian, 1978), 3–8, Kaufmann tells of his momentous decision as a youth of eleven to convert from Lutheranism to Judaism in Nazi Germany, much to his parents justified consternation. Some years later in the prologue of *Religions in Four Dimensions: Existential and Aesthetic, Historical and Comparative* (New York: Readers Digest Press, 1976), Kaufmann states that "Judaism in Nazi Germany was not merely a matter of reading about the past. It was an existential experience that involved my whole being."
5. Robert Proctor, *Education's Great Amnesia: Reconsidering the Humanities from Petrarch to Freud* (Bloomington: Indiana University Press, 1988).
6. Ibid., 110.
7. Ibid., 193.
8. Walter Kaufmann, ed., *Religion from Tolstoy to Camus* (New Brunswick, NJ: Transaction Publishers, 1994).
9. Walter Kaufmann, *Critique of Religion and Philosophy* (Princeton: Princeton University Press, 1958).
10. Walter Kaufmann, *Existentialism, Religion and Death: Thirteen Essays* (New York: Meridian, 1976).

11. *Judaism and Christianity: Essays by Leo Baeck*, trans. by Walter Kaufmann (Philadelphia: Jewish Publication Society of America, 1958).

12. Walter Kaufmann, *Religions in Four Dimensions*, 14–15.

13. Walter Kaufmann, *Goethe, Kant and Hegel: Discovering the Mind*, vol 1 (New Brunswick, NJ: Transaction Publishers, 1991), xix.

14. Roger Shattuck, "Perplexing Dreams: Is There a Core Tradition in the Humanities?" (Washington, DC: American Council of Learned Societies, 24 April 1987; ACLS Occasional Paper, No. 2., p. 8).

15. Irving Louis Horowitz, "The New Nihilism," *Society* 29, no. 1 (November/December 1991): 30.

16. See Kaufmann, *Faith of a Heretic*, chapter 2, "The Quest for Honesty."

17. Kaufmann, *Goethe, Kant and Hegel*, xvi.

18. Ibid., xvii.

19. Almost a decade later, Allan Bloom similarly recognized the effects of specialization: "Most professors are specialists, concerned only with their own fields, interested in the advancement of those fields in their own terms, or in their own personal advancement in a world where all the rewards are on the side of professional distinction," *The Closing of the American Mind* (New York: Simon and Schuster, 1987), 339.

20. Friedrich Nietzsche, *On the Genealogy of Morals and Ecce Homo*, trans. Walter Kaufmann (New York: Vintage Books, 1967), 147.

21. Stephen Graubard, in a somewhat disjointed keynote National Humanities Center address entitled, "The Agenda for the Humanities and Higher Education for the 21st Century" argues that the report of Vannevar Bush's *Science: The Endless Frontier* (1945) "might indeed provide a model for a humanities report in 1989" (p. 4). Much of his talk was devoted to a discussion of that model. Yet he is insightful in his contention that "the greatest loss of these last years may have been in the erosion of a sense of community," American Council of Learned Societies, ACLS Occasional Paper No. 8, 1989, p. 11. A recent conference of The New Jersey Committee for the Humanities, October 1993, was entitled, "The Culture of Community: The Importance of Community in American Life." A course on the culture of community could easily qualify as an interdisciplinary course under the criteria described by Kaufmann in the last chapter of *The Future of the Humanities*.

22. See *Nietzsche, Heidegger, and Buber: Discovering the Mind*, vol. 2 (New Brunswick, NJ: Transaction Publishers, 1992). Richard Rorty (Kaufmann's former colleague at Princeton University) and Kaufmann had long been at odds over the position of Heidegger's status in philosophy. Rorty states: "I do not think that you can tell much about the worth of a philosopher's views on topics such as truth, objectivity, and the possibility of a single vision by discover-

ing his politics, or his irrelevance to politics," "Trotsky and the Wild Orchids," in *Wild Orchids and Trotsky: Messages from American Universities*, ed. Mark Edmundson (New York: Penguin Books, 1993), 47.

23. That what is fashionable still persists on college campuses is easily confirmed. Mitchell Stephens, in an article entitled "Jacques Derrida," states that "[a]cademic departments that in the 1980's might have been looking to recruit a specialist in deconstruction now might be trying to outbid one another for some well-credentialed expert in 'gender studies' or 'gay studies,'" *The New York Times Magazine*, 23 January 1994, p. 25.

24. Kaufmann, *Religions in Four Dimensions*, 14.

25. The distinguished photographer André Kertész said of Professor Kaufmann's photography: "Professor Kaufmann's work is good, sensitive, intelligent, honest, and absolutely human. That is, to me, most important in photography."

26. Kaufmann, *Religions in Four Dimensions*, 18.

27. Ibid., 21.

28. One view on the subject of interdisciplinary studies holds that interdisciplinary thinking "is a sort of higher order commentary on the adequacy of a thought position already achieved, organized, and systematized," Allie Frazer, "The Interdisciplinary Heart of Liberal Studies," in *The Traditions in Modern Times: Graduate Liberal Studies Today*, ed. Charles B. Hands (Lanham, MD: University Press of America, 1988), 61. Kaufmann appears more radical: any thought position presupposes interdisciplinary work prior to its organization and systemization. Vlastos seems to concur with this position when he speaks of *Lernfreiheit* (interdepartmental study) in graduate education (Vlastos, "Graduate Education in the Humanities: Reflections and Proposals," in Frankena, *The Philosophy and Future of Graduate Education*, 76.

29. Walter Kaufmann, *Man's Lot: A Trilogy* (New York: Reader's Digest Press, 1978).

30. Kaufmann, *Faith of a Heretic*, 371–73.

PROLOGUE

The humanities are adrift. I have no desire to try to forecast where they may drift. My aim is not to predict but to influence their future.

The sad condition of the humanities should be a matter of vital concern for all of us. To be sure, what most people teaching and studying the humanities are doing is of little interest to nonspecialists. And much of what is taught and published is scarcely worth learning or reading. It is no wonder that many students have decided that college is a waste of time and that many parents are unsure whether it is not a waste of money. But there is a difference between what is being done and what could be done.

This difference is crucial not only for an evaluation of the humanities. It is all-important for humanity. We must reflect on what we might do, on our goals. And that is what the humanities should be about, although most teachers and students—especially in the humanities—seem to be unaware of this.

The humanities are in deep trouble. Those whose business is with higher education agree that something needs to be done. But as yet there has been insufficient discussion about what has gone wrong and about goals. My aim is to offer a diagnosis and a view of why and how the humanities should be taught. In the process it should become clear that what is at stake is nothing less than the future of humanity.

What exactly are "the humanities"? And is it really true that their condition is alarming? These questions must be answered briefly at the outset.

Six large fields are often referred to collectively as "the humanities": the study of religion and philosophy, art and music, literature and history. In colleges and universities the first four are usually pursued in separate departments, while literature is studied in many departments of which each is devoted to one language or group of languages, such as English or Romance Languages. These six fields are contrasted with the natural and social sciences. The humanities used to be considered rather more prestigious, but at least since the Second World War the natural sciences enjoy the greatest prestige and financial support, and the social sciences, though unable to point to any comparable accomplishments, bask in the reflected glory of being "scientific." Many historians would rather be considered social scientists than humanists, and so would many professors in other "humanities" departments. This is one of the problems that face the humanities.

Another problem has arisen only around 1970 but is much more threatening. It has suddenly become almost hopeless for young people with a doctorate in the humanities to find jobs as teachers. There are mainly two reasons for this. First, the steep rise in the birth rate during the forties (the so-called baby boom) did not last; the galloping growth of colleges and universities during the sixties came to an abrupt end; and after a period in which good graduate students were offered large salaries before they had even completed work on their doctorates because it was hard to find enough teachers, there ceased to be new openings. Second, so many positions, including professorships with permanent tenure, have been filled with young people that during the last quarter of the century few vacancies will be created by retirements. Both results were easy to predict but nevertheless took the academic establishment by surprise, and graduate schools have been extremely slow to adjust to the changed situation.

As recently as 1961 the retired head of the Carnegie Foundation for the Advancement of Teaching still argued in a book, *Graduate Education,* that the central problem was that the universities could not turn out enough Ph.D.'s to satisfy the needs of the seventies! He had just "visited some forty universities in search of the facts," and his chapter "The Growing Deficit in Ph.D.'s . . . " was crammed with figures—a symptom of the prestige of the sciences. Yet by 1975 there were two thousand American Ph.D.'s in philosophy alone who could not find teaching jobs, and the problem was worldwide.

On February 4, 1976, *The New York Times* reported (on page 38): "The latest figures from the United States Bureau of Labor Statistics' Division of Manpower and Occupation Outlook estimate that from 1972 to 1985 . . . prospects for doctoral graduates in the arts and humanities are . . . dismal, with 79,600 graduates expected to be available for 15,700 positions." More than 80 percent were not expected to find jobs of the kind for which they were trained.

The situation is especially acute in the arts and humanities because a doctorate in these fields has traditionally had no other function than to certify people for a teaching career in colleges and universities. Scientists with a Ph.D. usually have other, more lucrative, options as well. One might think of using the current surplus of Ph.D.'s to upgrade secondary school teaching; but the drop in the birth rate means that there are few openings at this level, too. Moreover, this innovation would close important job opportunities to young people without a Ph.D. Nor could we really upgrade secondary education in this way as long as the humanities are taught as they are taught at present. Most of our Ph.D.'s are not prepared at all to teach nonspecialist teenagers.

It follows that most graduate programs in the humanities will have to be curtailed drastically; many—preferably the least outstanding—will have to be abandoned altogether; most professors will have to give more attention to their undergraduates; and education in the humanities will have to be reconsidered.

Of course, the natural and social sciences would also profit from a close examination. Moreover, our educational problems begin at the secondary and primary school levels, or still earlier in the home and in the cultural environment that we provide. If only students entered college much better prepared than they are now, the outlook for higher education would be more promising. But a book dealing with the natural and social sciences as well as the humanities, and with grade schools and high schools no less than colleges and universities, would either have to be enormously long or hopelessly superficial. The field I hope to cover here is large enough, and even now I feel handicapped by an insufficient knowledge of music, for example, which I love without ever having had any halfway adequate training. To determine what in the social sciences is fakery and what might be fruitful is a big job that someone else should do; preferably a social scientist. And what could be done in the precollege years is too important a question to be considered briefly in the present context. There is a virtue in conciseness, and with that in mind I am not even including in these reflections the teaching of languages or of the creative arts. Both pose very different problems from the study of the six primary fields mentioned above. These six, on the other hand, involve similar problems, and the reasons for offering an education in these six are largely the same. It therefore makes sense to consider them together as "the humanities."

Plato showed long ago in the first major work ever written on education that one can deal with enduring problems and still be specific. I am interested in the larger questions but have tried throughout to be concrete, even to the point of making detailed suggestions for courses—as Plato did, too. In all such cases I have assumed that a term has ten weeks. In many schools it has more, which is all to the good and makes it possible to do more.

Another way of avoiding abstractness is to give illustrations and to name names as I do, for example, when distinguishing four kinds of minds in Chapter 1. Of course, it would be easier not to classify anyone in particular. As soon as one mentions individuals, one is bound to provoke contradiction and to make enemies. But the types take on flesh only as we deal with real people. To make matters worse, not everyone is familiar with the same names, and many readers will be baffled occasionally by an unfamiliar name. It would be a pity if anyone felt bothered by that. It would be more to the point for readers to ransack their own experience for striking illustrations.

The first chapter introduces more themes than could be followed up immediately. Instead of making amends by adding footnotes, I have tried to develop the major themes in the following chapters. The book forms a unit and needs to be considered as a whole.

It therefore had to be kept short, and I have eschewed any discussion of the immense literature on higher education. I stress the importance of considering objections and alternatives, and I generally try to practice what I preach. In earlier books I have usually given a great deal of space to my reasons for differing with other scholars; but in this book it seemed crucial to me to spell out a coherent view so concisely that others would be able to see it all at once without getting lost in arguments on relatively minor points.

For the same reason I have also refrained from giving more examples of what has gone wrong. While this might have made the book more entertaining, it would also have been a distraction. Most readers will have no trouble at all thinking of pitfalls *they* have seen. My aim is not to add to a long list but to show how many things fit together and what might be done about them.

2

The humanities are adrift. There are more than enough oarsmen, but most professors and students give little thought to goals. And if those in the humanities do not reflect on goals, who shall do it?

Some professors and students are busy playing games. More are analyzing games. Most of them are analyzing a few moves. Some do this very well, most of them not. But to ask about the point of their activities, their articles and books, their courses or their studies is considered uncouth.

Clichés about knowledge being its own reward and about following the truth wherever it may lead ignore the crucial question of priorities. Not all knowledge is equally rewarding. Nor do we encourage students and professors to spend years pursuing the truth about the father of the secretary of a man who ran unsuccessfully for Vicepresident of the United States. (It is no longer easy to think of examples on which some academic might not actually be working.)

Meanwhile, even some university presidents still speak of the humanities as if "humanistic" and "humanitarian" were synonyms. Although much of what is done in the field is clearly trivial, it is widely felt that the humanities may hold the key to the future of humanity. But as they are now taught all too often, they only hold the key to their own coffin.

The failure to think about goals is perilous in times of rapid change. When a ship has been at anchor for a long time without any thought of voyages, talk about goals may be dispensable. But when one is in constant motion and the views change all the time, the refusal to reflect on goals invites disaster.

The reasons for teaching the humanities are at least four. The first goal is the conservation and cultivation of the greatest works of humanity. By definition, the humanities deal with the history and achievements of humanity. But why should we occupy ourselves with past achievements? Much of history is utterly depressing, a ceaseless tale of human folly, blindness, and brutality. Yet not all this misery has been pointless; occasional triumphs redeem at least some of the suffering. Blessed with the priceless heritage of these rare triumphs, we should be traitors to humanity if we did not try to transmit it to generations to come.

Teaching the humanities should be an act of piety, prompted by reverence, but by no means only past-directed. One also hopes that Greek tragedy, Rembrandt, and Mozart may have a humanizing effect on the young. Is this merely a fond folly? After all, in Germany classical studies had flourished for more than a century before 1933, and Rembrandt and Mozart were widely esteemed. Inhumane aesthetes are as common as inhumane teachers of the humanities.

What matters is not only what is taught but also how it is taught and by what kinds of teachers. The humanizing effect is not too much to hope for if one brings to life the tragic poets, Rembrandt, and Mozart, confronting students with their humanity and their often extraordinary sensitivity to the feelings of others. Would this reduce teaching to preaching, and scholarship to edification? I hope to show in the chapter on the art of reading and in the discussion of translations how the approach I favor would be much more scholarly than most work done at present.

I strongly oppose any approach that reduces great writers or artists to mere mouthpieces for the interpreter's views. What makes most preaching tedious is this irreverent habit. Bringing to life great human beings of the past involves respect for them and their diversity. Students must be exposed to alternatives.

3

The second reason for teaching the humanities is related closely to this point. Philosophy and religion, literature and art deal in some measure with the ends of life, with possible goals of human existence, with our ultimate purposes. Those who believe that the right answers have been revealed once and for all and are clear beyond challenge may see no need for studying alternatives.

Actually, the persistent concern with alternatives developed two thousand years ago among rabbis who believed in revealed answers but who were also convinced that rival interpretations had to be considered. The medieval scholastics followed in their footsteps. In both cases, the alternatives that were considered fell within a consensus that was not questioned at the time but that most humanists today would question. The search for alternatives did not go far enough.

A thoughtful person should reflect on goals, giving attention to alternatives. As long as we fail to do this, we remain captives of a consensus and obey it blindly without ever having compared it with its rivals. The study of the humanities should be designed to liberate the mind and bring us closer to autonomy—to making fateful choices with our eyes open to alternatives.

The refusal of those teaching the humanities to face up to the question of their purposes is more serious than one might suppose. When security and certainty came to be sought through ever more specialization while the concern with goals and ends was disparaged, this vital concern lost its home in the academic world. Students were encouraged, in effect, to make the most important choices blindly, with their eyes closed to alternatives. There is much to be said in favor of specialization, and I shall try to show in Chapter 5 how specialized training is needed for autonomy. But it is important to realize how easily specialization can lead to myopia and even blindness.

The problem confronting the humanities received its classical formulation in the Sermon on the Mount: "If the salt have lost its savour, wherewith shall it be salted?" In most recent versions the savor of the King James Bible has been lost. *The New English Bible* actually asks, "how shall its saltness be restored?" If what is wanted is the spoken language, it would make more sense to render the Greek original thus: "When the salt becomes insipid, how can one salt it?"

The image of losing savor may suggest that things used to be good. But I do not mean to praise the past at the expense of the present, as if there had been more reflection on goals in my youth. Those who complain that the salt used to be saltier may be suspected of having lost their taste and of being old. And those who believe that past ages were not sick ought to study the humanities.

4

The third major reason for teaching the humanities is to teach vision. On the face of it, that may well seem to be impossible. In the strong sense of that word, only a few are visionaries; and any notion of turning every college student into a visionary is silly. The resolution of this problem depends on what is meant by vision.

In the first chapter I shall contrast visionaries in the strong sense of that term with three other human types that may be considered alternative models for professors and students. The next chapter deals with different ways of reading, for the art of reading is absolutely central in humanistic studies. These themes are pursued further in the discussion of reviews, translations, and editions in Chapter 3. Reviewers, translators, and editors are readers who influence the ways in which other people read. And people interested in books depend more and more on reviewers, translators, and editors.

Chapter 4 deals at length with one of the humanities, religion. If the point of humanistic studies is the preservation of the greatest works of humanity, reflection on alternative goals, and an attempt to make people less blind, then comparative religion must be given a central place in the humanities. For few works of literature can brook comparison with the Bible, the Dhammapada, or the Tao Teh Ching; and many of the greatest paintings, sculptures, buildings, and musical compositions originated in a religious context and cannot be fully understood apart from that. But little is gained by insisting on that unless one can show in some detail how comparative religion might be taught. Survey courses are always bound to be superficial in some ways, and hence such courses, much in favor at one time, have fallen into disrepute. It is therefore essential to be specific—and then to show how survey courses can and should be supplemented by intensive study of a single text. As an extended example I have chosen the Book of Genesis.

Then I shall return to the problem of how vision can be taught, and how specialization and discipline are essential for this purpose. The last chapter deals with ways of teaching, with courses and programs, and with the crucial role of interdisciplinary work.

In the modest sense of that word, all six chapters are part of a single "vision." Its basic elements have been spelled out here to show how the major pieces fit together. The typology in Chapter 1, for example, is not an end in itself but introduces the discussion of different ways of reading, and this in turn is developed further in relation to religious texts.

Any claim that one is communicating a vision sounds somewhat grandiloquent and may suggest that one lays claim to authority. My insistence on the need for studying alternatives should show that nothing could be further from my mind. We are adrift and must discuss goals. Here are some of mine, but I have never craved uncritical acceptance, nor do I think that a teacher should try to be as persuasive as possible. Affirmations without negations are empty, and I aim to present my views as alternatives, making plain what I negate. This raises more hackles than the manner of those who cite others mainly in support of their own views, giving the impression that all reasonable people are at one. But that is not the way to foster a critical spirit. And doing that is the fourth reason for teaching the humanities.

CHAPTER ONE:
FOUR
KINDS
OF MINDS

5

There are visionaries and scholastics. This distinction is essential for an understanding of the humanities as well as the natural and social sciences. No diagnosis of the ills of higher education should ignore this basic contrast.

Visionaries are loners. Alienated from the common sense of their time, they see the world differently and make sustained attempts to spell out their vision. Usually, they find existing languages inadequate, and often they encounter serious problems of communication.

Scholastics travel in schools, take pride in their rigor and professionalism, and rely heavily on their consensus or their common "know-how." They are usually hostile to contemporary visionaries, especially in their own field, but swear by some visionaries of the past.

In religion the visionaries are often called prophets and the scholastics priests. In philosophy and literature, history and the arts, there are no traditional terms for the two types, but sometimes the visionaries are called geniuses.

In science we have long had the contrast between the popular image of the mad scientist as a visionary and the positivists' very different notion of what it means to be scientific. In *The Structure of Scientific Revolutions* (1962) Thomas Kuhn has shown, in effect, how both visionaries and "normal" scientists function in the history of science. He described "normal science" as "puzzle-solving" within an accepted framework and then dealt with the emergence of scientific discoveries that lead to changes of world views. He did not deal primarily with human types and did not disparage what he called normal. On the contrary, he tried to show how needful the work of the industrious toilers is. The impact of his book has been immense.

More than a generation earlier, in 1918, Albert Einstein had delivered a brief address on the occasion of Max Planck's sixtieth birthday. By dividing the scholastic camp in two, he had recognized three types. There are those who "take to science out of a joyful sense of their superior intellectual power," people for whom science is a kind of "sport" that allows them to satisfy their ambition, while many others enter the temple of science "for purely utilitarian purposes. Were an angel of the Lord to come and drive all the people belonging to these two categories out of the temple," a few people would still be left, including Planck—"and that is why we love him."

This typology, unlike Kuhn's, is far from being value-free. It may even appear to be completely different from Kuhn's contrast and irrelevant to our purposes. For Einstein dealt with the psychological motives of research, although his address was later included in *Mein Weltbild,* and then also in several English collections of his essays, under the title "Principles of Research." But whatever *his* motive may have been, he left no doubt that his third type, the few like Planck, corresponds to our visionaries. For after conceding that it might be difficult in some cases to draw the line, he went on to say that he felt sure of one thing: "If the types we have just expelled were the only types there were, the temple would never have existed, any more than one can have a wood consisting of nothing but creepers."

Understandably, Einstein's typology did not have any very great immediate impact. It was not worked out in detail, and the disparagement of "creepers" could hardly have made it very popular.

It is noteworthy just how demanding Einstein's view was. Most readers of James D. Watson's brilliant and witty account of how he won the Nobel prize, *The Double Helix* (1968), were amazed to see how even some scientists of such distinction experience science as a kind of sport. And Watson went out of his way at almost every step to underline the vast distinction between those like him and Linus Pauling, the true visionary. Even so, Watson did not think of scientists of his own rank as essentially like the great mass of academics. He put the point succinctly when he explained in an educational television film, based on his book, why he felt instantly attracted by Francis Crick, who eventually shared the prize with him: Crick was not wasting his time; "most people are wasting their time." Though not quite as demanding as Einstein, Watson, too, evidently felt something like contempt for most scholastics. Kuhn, on the other hand, tried to show how the scholastics are needed.

Before we decide whether to keep our typology value-free, let us trace back the fundamental contrast beyond Einstein, to Goethe. Goethe was not only the greatest German poet but also a remarkable scientist. In his *Doctrine of Colors (Farbenlehre,* 1810), which he himself considered as important as any of his works, he argued against Newton.

Even those who have no doubt that *Einstein* scored against Newton generally take for granted that Goethe did not, and that Goethe's *Doctrine of Colors* can be safely ignored. Yet this work has merits that are quite independent of the question whether Goethe or Newton was right about colors.

Goethe pioneered a humanistic approach to science. In his beautifully written preface he said:

> We compare the Newtonian color theory with an old castle that was initially planned by its builder with youthful haste, but by and by amplified by him and furnished in accordance with the needs of the time and circumstances and, in the course of skirmishes and hostilities, fortified and secured more and more.

Goethe went on to describe how the castle was gradually enlarged as one "added towers, baywindows, and battlements," as well as ever so many other features. All the while

> one venerated the old castle because it had never been conquered, because it had repulsed so many attacks, frustrated so many enemies, and retained its virginity. This claim, this reputation still endures. Nobody notices that the old building has become uninhabitable.

Surprisingly, perhaps, it was by no means Goethe's central purpose to show that his own doctrine was true and Newton's false, nor even to replace the "old castle" with his own edifice.

> If we should succeed by the use of our utmost power and skill to reduce this bastille [that is, to bring off a scientific revolution] and to gain a free space, it is by no means our intention to cover it up and molest it again right away with a new building. We prefer to use it in order to present a series of beautiful forms.
>
> The third part is therefore devoted to historical investigations and preliminaries. If we said above that the history of

man shows us man, one could now claim that the history of science is science itself. One cannot gain pure recognition of what one possesses until one knows what others have possessed before us. One will not truly and honestly enjoy the advantages of one's own time if one does not know how to appreciate the advantages of the past. But to write a history of the doctrine of color . . . was impossible as long as the Newtonian doctrine held the field. For no aristocratic conceit has ever looked down with as much intolerable arrogance upon those who did not belong to the same guild, as the Newtonian school has always condemned everything that was achieved before or beside it.

What concerns us here is not Goethe's quarrel with Newton, who was, like Goethe, one of the greatest visionaries of all time, but rather Goethe's critique of the Newtonian school—of the scholastics. In 1829 he returned to this theme in a short essay that was published only posthumously, in 1833, under the title "Analysis and Synthesis":

A false hypothesis is better than none at all, for that it is false does no harm at all; but when it fortifies itself, when it is accepted universally and becomes a kind of creed that nobody may doubt, that nobody may investigate, that is the disaster of which centuries suffer.

The Newtonian doctrine could be presented; even in his own time its defects were urged against it, but the man's other great merits and his position in the social and scholarly world did not allow contradiction to gain any standing. The French especially are to be blamed more than anyone else for the spread and ossification of this doctrine. In the nineteenth century they should therefore make up for this mistake by favoring a fresh analysis of this intricate and frozen hypothesis.

Goethe introduced so many pertinent themes in unforgettable images that it seemed best to let him speak at some length. (Translations in this book are always mine.)

Here is an archvisionary putting his case against scholasticism—prompted not by pique but by concern for the freedom of the human spirit. He pioneered a new humanistic discipline, the history of science, and rejected the dogmatic faith in cumulative progress that was widely shared until Kuhn's *Structure of Scientific Revolutions* called it into question more than a century and a half later. Of course, the theme of discontinuity and the insight that science is a human endeavor alongside poetry and music, history and philosophy, art and religion, were prominent in Hegel's thought as well as Nietzsche's; but in the English-speaking world they have gained ground only since World War II.

Legions of professors and students in the humanities have accepted "science" as a model while still sharing the positivistic faith in cumulative progress. But Goethe knew that his own scientific discoveries were not altogether different from his work as a poet; both involved vision; and the history of science, as he conceived it, placed science in a human context.

In another work I hope to show how this Goethean conception remained alive in Germany and how it helps us understand not only Hegel and Nietzsche but also existentialism and psychoanalysis. Kuhn's debt to this tradition is indirect but nevertheless unmistakable and openly acknowledged. And the rapid spread of history of science programs on our campuses since World War II is one of the few hopeful developments in the humanities during the past decades.

6

My contrast of visionaries and scholastics represents a variation on an old theme. It can be developed in one of two ways. We can follow Einstein's lead and think of the visionaries as a few people including Planck—as well as

Einstein and Goethe, Beethoven and Michelangelo, Plato and Moses. These visionaries did not yield to anyone in craftsmanship. If we contrast people of this type with scholastics who, by definition, do not have great visions of their own, the dichotomy becomes somewhat Manichaean, with all good on one side.

To avoid that, one could expand the category of the visionaries to include crackpots. One could insist that both visionaries and scholastics can be "good" or "bad." Visionaries can have fixed ideas that they back up with ingenious arguments; they can be obsessional or paranoiac and often are both; even the greatest visionaries sometimes are of this type at least some of the time—Newton, for example—and most people of this type lack Newton's genius.

One could even go further and insist that people with distinctive world views are quite common in asylums, that hallucinations are visions of a sort, and that Goethe and his kind represent no more than one type of visionary and a very small minority of the whole class. The virtue of this approach is that it is by no means Manichaean or simplistic. Its disadvantage is that it encumbers us with types that are of no great interest in connection with the future of the humanities.

Of course, there is a multitude of human types, and a scholastic might have a great time noting subclasses and making fine distinctions. For our purposes, however, it will be most fruitful to stick to the definitions given at the outset. Sustained attempts to spell out a distinctive vision—and that is part of my definition—require a mastery of technique. Those who have visions but lack the power to articulate them in a sustained way are of no concern to us here. It follows that what distinguishes the scholastic from the visionary is not rigor but reliance on consensus and the lack of a distinctive vision.

It does not follow that all visionaries are "good," all

scholastics "bad." Not every distinctive vision is plausible, beautiful, or fruitful. And it may require the concerted efforts of a great many scholastics to work out the details of a vision before we can judge its value.

Nietzsche was right when he said in a posthumously published note: "The first adherents prove nothing *against* a doctrine." Freud had ample reasons to agree with that, and yet, for all of his dissatisfaction with his followers, he needed them to test his theories. He was a visionary; he did make a sustained attempt to spell out his vision; and he kept testing it by both continued self-analysis and his analysis of patients, as well as a good deal of reading. But he knew that all this was not enough; he also needed scholastics.

In sum, many visionaries do have fixed ideas that are not particularly fruitful; and many scholastics are by no means unimaginative drudges but perform tasks that are badly needed. The great visionary whose technical virtuosity compels our wonder does not have to be considered a mixed type. But there are intermediate types—scholastics who belong to a school and rely on its consensus but who also try to spell out some perceptions of their own. The size of this perception may vary, but in those who are not visionaries it falls short of a comprehensive vision that amounts to an alternative to the consensus. What people of this type see is often merely a new way of supporting the consensus of their school. In Einstein's words, it may be "a pretty ticklish job" in some cases to draw the line, but generally people of this type are best considered as scholastics. So far, then, we have two fundamental types.

7

Some periods are more scholastic than others. Scholasticism prevails whenever the leading figures in a field are to be found at schools, at colleges or universities.

Originally, the term "scholastics" referred to medieval philosophers who taught at schools, belonged to schools of thought, prized subtlety and rigor, and depended heavily on a consensus that they did not question. In many ways most twentieth-century philosophers—and professors in other fields as well—resemble them.

In the seventeenth and eighteenth centuries, however, the most memorable philosophers were visionaries who neither taught nor belonged to any school of thought; notably Francis Bacon, Hobbes, and Descartes; Spinoza, Locke, and Leibniz; Berkeley, Hume, and Rousseau. Kant was the first great modern philosopher who was a professor.

Kant was a visionary, but nobody could have known it until he was fifty-seven and had held a chair for eleven years. In many ways he was as timid as his vision was bold, and he had a terrible time trying to communicate his vision in a book. When he finally did, his prose looked like a parody of scholasticism. He seemed anxious to be more pedantic than the German schoolmen of his century and the scholastics of the Middle Ages. But his German successors quickly adopted his manner, and soon Hegel perfected the parody. In the nineteenth century most philosophers were professors, and many tried to write like Kant and Hegel. In our own time, many philosophers and literary critics, as well as some social scientists still do; for example, Jean-Paul Sartre in his philosophical tomes.

If we could only classify Kant and Hegel as scholastics, we would avoid a dichotomy in which all genius is on one side. In defense of such a move one could point out that both at times supported a consensus. Yet we cannot begin to understand either of these men until we see how each had a distinctive and exceptionally comprehensive vision that was importantly different from any consensus of their time. Neither of them relied on the agreement of professional colleagues or on a method shared by fellow workers in the field. Both were loners and spent their most creative years on a sustained attempt to spell out their visions.

Their scholastic critics and interpreters often fail to understand that Kant and Hegel felt sure they were right not so much on account of one or another argument but rather because they thought that they could see how all the major parts of their philosophies were connected and supported one another. It was partly for this reason that Kant did not take kindly to the well-meant suggestion that he might attenuate his moral rigorism to make his ethic gentler and a little more humane. The rigorism was required by what Hegel, a generation later, would have called "the system."

In the nineteenth century there were still a few major philosophers who were not professors of philosophy: John Stuart Mill and Nietzsche, for example. But in the twentieth century philosophy as well as the study of art, music, and religion, literature, and history became almost wholly academic. Since World War II ever more artists and poets, composers and novelists, have become academics, too. And most professors are scholastics.

8

It may seem to be an inevitable consequence of higher education for the masses that almost all the teachers have to be scholastics. The more students one tries to educate reasonably well, the more teachers one needs, and visionaries are rare.

Moreover, most visionaries require a good deal of solitude to retain a firm hold on their distinctive vision, and they generally prefer their creative work to teaching large numbers of students. Conversely, when they do immerse themselves in academic life and try to get along with large numbers of colleagues and students, they tend to become more and more scholastic.

A visionary could hardly feel at home in the academic milieu, as Spinoza knew when he declined an invitation to become a professor at Heidelberg, as Nietzsche found out before he resigned his chair of classical philology at Basel, and as Wittgenstein found out at Cambridge University. Those who neither decline nor resign are tempted constantly to make concessions to the prevalent scholasticism.

The consensus of the scholastics differs drastically from one school to another but is usually intolerant because one cannot concentrate on playing a game well if the rules are questioned continually. The visionary calls into question the whole framework within which the scholastics are trying to solve various puzzles. Or, to develop Einstein's metaphor, the visionary marks for chopping down the trees on which the creepers climb and thrive.

"Creepers" is a term with disparaging overtones that suggests the hostility of a great visionary to a caste he did not love. Synonyms have different associations but are hardly friendlier: "climbers," for example, or "ramblers." The German word Einstein used was *Schlingpflanzen*—plants that coil around trees like giant snakes that suffocate or crush their prey. *Schlingen* also means devouring greedily, and Einstein's total image shows how he thought of the creepers or climbers as parasites.

It is no wonder then that the scholastics should feel threatened by the visionaries—excepting those on whom they depend for their sustenance. The hostility is mutual. And it would be utterly unrealistic to suppose that visionaries generally are like Einstein. His charm and his humanity were as extraordinary as his genius.

The visionaries whom a school might consider hiring or promoting are almost always of an altogether different order of magnitude. Those who play the games favored by a given department, abide by the rules, and play exceptionally well can be judged highly competent. Those who disdain some of the rules or engage in altogether different enterprises, while considering the games played by the department with indifference or contempt, may simply be unsound, undisciplined, and incompetent. It is much less likely that one or another of these people has a vision that it would be worthwhile adding to one's offerings. The odds are against that. The safest procedure in hiring and promotions is to stick to what one knows well and can judge.

If a department is very broad-minded and eager to present its students with two or more alternatives, it will still be safer not to take a chance on visionaries. The obvious thing to do is to hire scholastics who belong to another school of thought and are recommended as highly competent representatives of that school. As a result, teachers who question the consensus of the dominant schools of thought in college departments are not likely to be hired or promoted unless they belong to rival schools of thought that have gained a wide following and therefore also respectability. Visionaries, being loners, do not stand much of a chance in academia.

To quote the conclusion of a short poem, "The Academic Zoo," from my *Cain and Other Poems:*

> Whatever spins web or cocoon
> is welcome, however jejune.
>> Butterfly
>> need not apply.

For the reasons given, this is not surprising. But it is startling at times to see how scholastics bury their own prophet under appreciations of the kind he loathed; how little feeling they show, more often than not, for his spirit; and how oblivious they are as a rule to his opinion of the games they play.

That Wittgenstein is a striking case in point is well known. Kierkegaard is another. It is not enough to note that most of those who write about him, or who translate him, appear to have no feeling for his mordant humor. Nor is it sufficient to imagine how he might have satirized the parsons and professors who contribute to the literature about him. Naturally, our university presses, who bear the brunt of scholarly publishing, must accept solid and stolid studies about Kierkegaard that he himself would have detested, provided only that such manuscripts are truly scholarly—as Kierkegaard was not. But suppose for a moment that Kierkegaard had submitted *The Concept of Dread* or *The Sickness unto Death,* or any number of his other books, to a good university press. They would certainly have been rejected.

Anyone as innovative, eccentric, and provocative as Kierkegaard could hardly hope to "make it" in the academic world. That is as true in our time as it was in Kierkegaard's. But even in the case of Kierkegaard, which is particularly glaring, few of the scholastics who have gathered round him seem to have much sense of that.

This contrast between visionaries and "creepers" is surely one of the most pervasive features of the life—or is it the death?—of the spirit. It is the curse of religion and one of the staples of humanities departments. William Butler Yeats, perhaps the greatest poet in the English language in this century, dealt with it in a twelve-line poem called

The Scholars

Bald heads forgetful of their sins,
Old, learned, respectable bald heads
Edit and annotate the lines
That young men, tossing on their beds,
Rhymed out in love's despair . . .
All think what other people think. . . .

This is not Yeats at his best, and he dulls the point by contrasting the old and young. If that were all, I should not dwell on the point here. A cynic might even suggest that this is not such a bad occupation for the old. But today most scholastics are young, and most of them make sure that their students and readers "think what other people think."

Those who have never been upset by all this do not know the poverty of higher education. It is easy to shut one's eyes to it and dwell on what looks good, or to laugh at the farce and drown in resignation. Yet all this is *not* inevitable. The dualistic typology presented so far is inadequate. We have to introduce a third type.

9

Socrates was no scholastic. He was a loner and questioned the common sense of his time. Yet he did not try to spell out a vision of his own. He made a point of not being a visionary and of being, in effect, an antischolastic. He examined the faith and morals of his time, ridiculed claims to knowledge that were based on an uncritical reliance on consensus, and exerted himself to show how ignorant, confused, and credulous most people are—including the most famous teachers, politicians, and popular oracles. Thus *Socrates embodied a third type.*

The most striking feature of this type is its concentration on criticism. But if I spoke of *critics,* visionaries, and scholastics, this might invite the misapprehension that most so-called critics who write about art and music, literature and films, exemplify this type. In fact, some are scholastics, and most of them are journalists.

Journalism is a profession, like teaching; and if we think of journalists in this sense, they are obviously not all of one type. But it may be useful to define *the journalist as a fourth type,* in line with the literal meaning of the term. So understood, the journalist writes for the day, for instant consumption, knowing that his wares have to be sold now or never because they will be stale tomorrow. He has no time for extensive research and no taste for the scholastics' rigor. Footnotes are not for him, while scholastics frequently discover when they check their sources once more to add footnotes that their facts require some correction. Hence scholastics, no less than visionaries, often feel contempt for journalists.

In his stage directions, near the beginning of Act IV of *The Doctor's Dilemma,* Bernard Shaw describes a journalist as

> a cheerful, affable young man who is disabled for ordinary business pursuits by a congenital erroneousness which renders him incapable of describing accurately anything he sees, or understanding or reporting accurately anything he hears. As the only employment in which these defects do not matter is journalism... , he has perforce become a journalist. . . .

If possible, Byron was even nastier in "English Bards and Scotch Reviewers" (lines 976ff.) when he spoke of

> A monthly scribbler of some low lampoon,
> Condemn'd to drudge, the meanest of the mean,
> And furbish falsehoods for a magazine, . . .
> Himself a living libel on mankind.

In Nietzsche's recurrent polemics against journalism we encounter another motif that is as important for the future of the humanities now as it was in his time. On January 16, 1872, he delivered the first of six public lectures in Basel, "On the Future of Our Educational Institutions." Near the end of this lecture he contrasted "the journalist, the servant of the moment," with the genius whom he called rather romantically "the redeemer from the moment." The theme sounded here at the beginning of Nietzsche's career is varied a year later in the brilliant title of his *Untimely Meditations.*

What is at stake for Nietzsche is his own vision of the philosopher as "a man of tomorrow and the day after tomorrow" who must stand "in contradiction to his today" (*Beyond Good and Evil,* section 212). Philosophers, he goes on to say, should be "the bad conscience of their time." And then Socrates is described as an exemplary philosopher who was a ruthless critic of his age.

Our concern here is with the humanities, whose point it is, at least in part, to provide us with perspectives on our time. This theme will have to be developed at length later on, but it must be introduced at the outset because in this way the ethos of the humanities is diametrically opposed to that of the journalist as a type. But for the present let us return to Shaw.

Shaw made an important point, though I take exception to "congenital erroneousness." The attitude in question is not really congenital but inculcated.

I remember being interviewed for a student newspaper when I was an undergraduate, newly arrived from Nazi Germany. I was appalled by what struck me as utterly pointless inaccuracies and especially the young man's defense of his placing in quotes all sorts of statements I had not made. He assured me that quotation marks made things more interesting and that it was important to break up a story every now and then with quotes.

The ethos of the journalist as a type, alongside the visionary, scholastic, and Socratic type, is to provide copy that looks interesting and readable at first blush but is not expected to stand up on close examination, much less a few years later. This ethos is widespread enough to be worth discussing here; and many of us also know people who exemplify this ethos in conversation.

Many professors in the humanities as well as the sciences consider it an important part of their job to wean their students from this dirty habit and housebreak them. In this respect many scholastic and Socratic teachers are at one.

When we read stories in even the best of newspapers about events that we have personally witnessed, we find almost always that there are many inaccuracies and that the reporter's or the editor's attitude was not far different from that of the undergraduate journalist. Having read Shaw, one is frequently reminded of his comments. But people who make lists of the leading intellectuals of their society and end up largely with the names of people who either edit or contribute frequently to journals are not thinking of reporters.

This is a touchy point, but it will not do to avoid it; for role models are all-important. There is a continuum all the way from the undergraduate reporter to the highest regions of journalism, and the only names worth mentioning are those at the top.

10

Perhaps no twentieth-century American journalist was more widely regarded as a leading intellectual than Edmund Wilson, who for a long time was a regular contributor to *The New Yorker* and then, toward the end of his life, to *The New York Review of Books*. What some people consider his greatest work, *To the Finland Station* (1940), initially appeared in part in the pages of *The New Republic;* and on checking his report on Hegel I found that his "knowledge" was clearly secondhand and quite wrong, and the sections on Marx not much better.

It may be objected that Wilson was after all mainly a literary critic. But when we turn to what is perhaps his most highly regarded collection of essays in literary criticism, *The Wound and the Bow* (1941), the picture is essentially the same. The title of the book alludes to Sophocles' *Philoctetes,* but the conclusion of the book shows how carelessly Wilson had read this tragedy. He claims that the nobility of Neoptolemus, which he describes at length, "dissolves

Philoctetes' stubbornness, and thus cures him and sets him free, and saves the campaign as well"—and this remained unchanged in the "new printing with corrections" in 1947 (page 295; see also 283). In fact, Philoctetes is not at all persuaded by Neoptolemus to abandon his resentment, and it requires a *deus ex machina,* Heracles, to intervene from above and ordain that Philoctetes has to become the savior of his people. (I shall show in the next chapter how really crucial this difference is.)

Wilson's summary of Sophocles' *Antigone* is no less reminiscent of Shaw's charges, down to Shaw's insistence that journalists always seem to get names wrong. Even the "new printing, with corrections" abounds in errors, and Creon is consistently called Cleon. Cleon was a famous Athenian politician and a contemporary of Sophocles, not of Antigone.

Journalistically, Wilson's *The Scrolls from the Dead Sea* (1955), initially serialized in *The New Yorker,* was a great coup that did much to call public attention to one of the most significant discoveries of our time. But to say that the book did not look very good twenty years later would be much too charitable. Once again, Shaw came much closer to the mark, though Wilson's trouble was in part that he listened to the wrong people.

It is important to note that this point does not concern merely one writer. The book that made Hannah Arendt very famous was unquestionably *Eichmann in Jerusalem* (1963), which was initially written for *The New Yorker.* There has been a great deal of discussion about the theses of the book; for example, about her notion of "the banality of evil," which many critics have found quite offensive. I have no wish here to continue these arguments. That thesis in particular I had tried to formulate in a short trilogy, "The Eichmann Trial," included in *Cain and Other Poems* (1962). The second poem begins:

He looks like a mouse, not like a great cat;
he is thoroughly unromantic.
He is proud that he was bureaucrat,
and he is still pedantic.

Why can't a monster be big and black?
Some like administration,
and what creates hell is sometimes a lack
of feeling and imagination. . . .

The point was not new and is to be found, for example, in Tolstoy's magnificent short story "After the Ball," which I read only later.

This issue needs to be mentioned here because anyone finding fault with Arendt's facts is almost always assumed right away to be concerned to demolish her theses. Nothing could show better how much most people have been corrupted by the journalistic ethos. Even if Arendt's other theses had been as tenable as this one is to my mind, it should still have been a major scandal that a person who ostensibly was above all a scholar and a leading humanist should have come as close to Shaw's description as she did.

Seeing Arendt as a journalist illuminates her earlier books, too. They were not written for journals and not so *obviously* journalistic. Indeed, her first major work, *The Origins of Totalitarianism* (1951), was impressively erudite. Yet scholars have never taken seriously her suggestion that the origins of totalitarianism must be found in anti-Semitism and imperialism, to which Arendt had devoted the first two-thirds of the book. Actually, she talked about evils that were constantly in the news and regularly condemned, and the title of her book was little more than a catchy headline.

Arendt never even noted that the single most important source of totalitarianism was the Inquisition, which she totally ignored along with Plato's *Republic* and the Nocturnal Council in his *Laws*. She did mention the *Laws* once, saying

that "Plato invoked Zeus ... in his *Laws*" and implying
rather oddly that Plato was the first who "understood that
laws are the stabilizing forces in the public affairs of men."
In fact, that insight coupled with the invocation of a god can
be traced back beyond Hammurabi, who lived roughly four-
teen centuries before Plato. Moreover, Dostoevsky had
shown in "The Grand Inquisitor" in *The Brothers
Karamazov* how totalitarianism is compatible with the invocation of God. But Arendt never mentioned this most brilliant analysis of totalitarianism, which was familiar to the
Bolshevik revolutionaries. (For a more detailed account of
the relevant aspects of the Inquisition, see my *Religions in
Four Dimensions,* section 52.) Arendt liked to deal
breathlessly with what was topical, and she lacked more
than soundness. She had far less understanding of totalitarianism and of the behavior of the victims, with which she
dealt at length in her Eichmann book, than is to be found in
the books of Alexander Solzhenitsyn.

Journalism and scholasticism may seem to be opposites.
The scholastic values rigor and being sound, the journalist
speed and being interesting. Yet there are journalistic
scholastics—professors who write for journals, which may
range all the way from *The New Yorker* to so-called scholarly journals. And what, it may be asked, is wrong with that?

Nothing. Not all people who are journalists by profession
belong to the type under consideration here; much less do all
people who sometimes write for journals. What matters is
the ethos.

Those who make a living writing for a journal can have
the highest standards of accuracy, though this would be sure
to make their life very hard. And some who never write for
journals have very little intellectual integrity. Moreover,
sometimes—although much more rarely than most people
seem to think—speed is indeed of the essence, and a report
must be published in a hurry without time for much checking and double-checking.

What needs to be noted is that the ethos of those who do not care how the things they fashion in a hurry will stand up in thirty years is very different from that of a historian like Thucydides who had the ambition to create "a possession for all time," or a philosopher like Nietzsche who hoped to be "born posthumously." Many scholastics write on timely topics for scholarly journals, making a great show of rigor, although they have no hope whatsoever that their publications might endure for thirty years, or even ten; and upon close inspection the rigor is often merely apparent and the wares are as shoddy as at first glance they seemed solid.

The journalistic orientation poses an immense threat to the future of the humanities. Some old-fashioned humanists felt that whatever was not worth reading ten times was not worth reading at all. They concentrated on books that had survived for centuries, and they ignored what seemed ephemeral—often even science, because it kept changing. The predilection of journalistic teachers for what is "news" and their concern with the latest fads endangers the conservation of the greatest works of the human spirit. More and more students graduate from college having read a lot of recent articles and books that but a short while later are as dated and forgotten as are most of last year's headlines. Meanwhile, even art historians rarely know the Bible.

11

It should be clear why I speak of the Socratic type and not of critics. If we spoke of critics, we would have to distinguish at least two types: the Socratic and the journalistic critic. These two are plainly antithetical.

Socrates insisted that his wisdom consisted in his awareness of his ignorance, while most of those considered wise in his time claimed to know what in fact they did not know. It was part of his mission, as he himself defined it according to the *Apology,* to expose the ignorance of those who were considered wise and the spuriousness of their claims to knowledge.

The journalist, as defined here, claims to know what he does not know—and in some cases even what he knows not to be so, as when he places statements in quotation marks because that looks more interesting. Socrates maintained that even the most pious and defensible beliefs could never justify confusions or bad arguments. What he impressed upon posterity, by way of some of Plato's works in which he appears as a character, was the need for intellectual integrity. But when we examine his own arguments closely, we find that he often fell short of his own standards, sometimes because he enjoyed making fools of others.

What I mean by the Socratic type is the type committed to the rigorous examination of the faith and morals of the time, giving pride of place to those convictions which are widely shared and rarely questioned. Reliance on consensus and prestigious paradigms are prime targets. There may be an element of perversity in all this. However that may be, for people of this type it is a point of honor to swim against the stream.

There have been many famous visionaries, and scholastics as well as journalists come in large numbers. But Socrates may have been the only very famous exemplar of the unalloyed Socratic type. Later teachers of this kind have found no Plato. Teachers who have no vision of their own and do not write are often fondly and admiringly remembered by their students without attaining lasting fame.

It is crucially important to recognize this type as a viable alternative to the visionary and scholastic. Most teachers will never achieve lasting fame in any case, and many, after due reflection on the main alternatives, might well opt for this ethos.

Moreover, the Socratic tendency has appeared in a variety of blends. In fact, as soon as we assume that many teachers and writers combine two tendencies, our four kinds of minds yield *sixteen types*. There are not only four pure types, but each also appears in conjunction with each of the three others. If we use a 1 to stand for the visionary type, a 2 for the Socratic type, a 3 for the scholastic, and a 4 for the journalist, the sixteen types could be represented as follows: 11, 12, 13, 14; 22, 21, 23, 24; 33, 31, 32, 34; 44, 41, 42, 43. Some might not care to distinguish between 12 (the visionary with a Socratic element) and 21 (the Socratic type with a visionary element). If we dropped this kind of distinction, we could eliminate six types and reduce the list to ten. But it would be a pity to do that, as a few examples may show.

11. the more or less pure visionary: Blake and Yeats.
12. Plato, Nietzsche, Freud; Euripides, Tolstoy; Goya.
13. Aristotle, Kant, Hegel.
14. Toynbee, Bertrand Russell's *A History of Western Philosophy*.

22. Socrates.
21. Lessing, Shaw, Heinrich Böll; Daumier, George Grosz.
23. many professors.
24. Kierkegaard, Karl Kraus. This blend makes for self-hatred.

33. compilers of dictionaries, concordances, scholarly editions.
31. Aquinas.
32. G. E. Moore and many other professors.
34. Tillich and many other professors.

44. most journalists and authors of bestsellers.
41. Edmund Wilson and Hannah Arendt?
42. David Susskind.
43. Charles Reich's *The Greening of America*.

One could have a great deal of fun arguing about individual cases, including some of the people I have classified as well as legions of others. One could also note that some famous people blend three types, and that Jean-Paul Sartre has strong elements of all four. To realize what a scholastic could do with this typology, one only needs to recall Polonius' words to Hamlet:

> The best actors in the world, either for tragedy, comedy, history, pastoral, pastoral-comical, historical-pastoral, tragical-historical, tragical-comical-historical-pastoral . . .

For our purposes it will be quite sufficient to distinguish four kinds of minds, provided we recall that pure types are the exception. Moreover, one might suppose that while journalists and visionaries can be found in many fields, only philosophers can be scholastic or Socratic. This short list shows at a glance how philosophers have no monopoly on either type. The Socratic probing of the faith and morals of the age and the Socratic ridicule of the most celebrated oracles—including those it is not fashionable to attack—are not by any means prerogatives of the philosophers. To be sure, philosophy could contribute a great deal along this line, but so can novelists and poets, artists and teachers in other fields—as well as men and women who are by profession journalists.

12

Recognition of these four types could make a tremendous difference in higher education. It is pointless to criticize scholastics for not being visionaries. Such criticism is sterile and can hardly produce innovation. Moreover, a faculty consisting largely of visionaries would be a nightmare. But one can fault a faculty for being insufficiently Socratic and for not communicating the Socratic ethos to its students.

It is essential for us to realize that being a scholastic is not the only respectable alternative to being a great visionary.

The Socratic option is not often spelled out clearly, but when something of the sort is done, the scholastics sometimes plead that this is not their job.

This is a very curious notion. Its obvious meaning is: This is not what we get paid for. There is some truth in that.

Academic freedom developed in the nineteenth century in Germany, where the professors were civil servants, paid by the state. They were granted "academic" freedom, meaning that they were free to teach their subject matter as they wished, provided they refrained from questioning the faith, morals, and politics of their society. Their freedom was thus strictly academic; and being Socratic was emphatically not what they were paid for.

In a sense, then, the retort that this is not our job is true. But only the meanest hirelings will be content—or should be content—to tailor their conception of their task as professors to the wishes of the state or those from whom the money comes with which they happen to be paid. More than almost anybody else, tenured professors can define their own job, and they are in an excellent position to persuade society of their conception of their task. Actually, it is the professors to whom we owe the current prestige of the scholastic conception. It is the professors who have sold this conception to the public, without ever reflecting deeply on alternatives.

The claim that the cultivation of a Socratic ethos is not their job must be met with the following questions. First: Is the job worth doing? And then, if it is worth doing: Is there any other group that is better qualified by training and position to do it? And finally, if there is not: Are we doing something so much more important that it would be irresponsible of us to take on this job?

Let us try to answer all three questions, beginning with the first: Is the job worth doing? The best approach to it is concrete and historical.

13

Through the first third of this century, Germany was a model of higher education and professionalism. Many Americans went to German universities to obtain a Ph.D., and the American graduate schools, which are still with us in the last third of the century, were developed in the German image. In the 1920s physicists from all over the world went to Göttingen to study there.

In the 1930s the German universities became the perfect paradigm of the moral bankruptcy of pure professionalism. Most of the leading German scholars failed to question the faith, morals, and politics of their society. After all, that was not their job. It was not what they got paid for. And their students, taught by internationally famous scholars, were even more uncritically enthusiastic about the new faith, morals, and politics of the Nazi state than their less educated fellow citizens. The students had never been taught to apply to faith, morals, and politics the standards of conscientiousness of which scholastics are so proud. On the contrary, they had been taught a kind of two-world doctrine, and faith and morals—or in one word, values—were believed to be immune against critical scrutiny. The domain of values had become a refuge for prejudice and passion.

The two dominant Western philosophies of the 1920s— existentialism and positivism—are still dominant half a century later. Although they may seem to be diametrically opposite and their partisans see them as antithetical, both schools agree in their profoundly, but extremely unprofound, anti-Socratic ethos. Both confine reason to the world of facts and leave the realm of faith, morals, and politics to emotion, passion, and irrational decisions.

This anti-Socratic ethos need not put on philosophic airs. Legions of professors who would never call themselves positivists or existentialists still share the consensus that their job is to teach their specialty, and that academic competence and excellence depend on more and ever more specialization. Our modern scholastics often insist that faith and morals are best left to preachers. But on reflection this makes no sense. What special expertise do preachers have? Why should we listen to them? Where scholars fear to tread, demagogues rush in.

Socrates' job needs doing. The conflicting faiths, moral codes, and ideologies of our time badly need thoughtful examination. No group is better qualified and in a better position to do this job than the tenured faculties of colleges and universities. If they have no time for the Socratic task, it is idle to hope that the job will be done well elsewhere.

14

The question remains whether the job actually done by most professors teaching the humanities is more important. If so, it might still be the lesser evil to leave Socrates' job undone. People who are not professors might well say that the very question is ridiculous and that what most professors teaching the humanities are doing is downright trivial by comparison. But people who are not scholars may not be reliable judges of what is trivial and what is not.

It seems reasonable to distinguish form and content at this point. The content of much work in the humanities *is,* I think, trivial compared to the Socratic undertaking; but the discipline acquired in the course of such work can nevertheless be invaluable. This is an important point that will require more attention in the chapter ''Vision Can Be Taught, But. . . . ''

The question facing us is not whether it would be better for all professors to be scholastics or for all of them to be Socratic. Since World War II our faculties have become more and more scholastic, and the question is whether we can afford the extinction of the Socratic ethos. I am arguing that we cannot, but this obviously does not commit me to the notion that it would be best if this were the only type represented on our faculties. Those who plead against the extinction of whales are not implying that it would be best if there were nothing but whales in the oceans.

Of course, my interest in the survival of the Socratic type is prompted by a deep concern not for mere variety but for the future of the humanities. The point is not that it would be a great pity if we had one type less than we used to have; it is rather that *the humanities require a mix in which the Socratic type is an indispensable ingredient.*

One might compare the Socratic ethos to salt or pepper, suggesting that without it the diet becomes flat and tasteless, although a diet of nothing but salt or pepper would be worse. But this image is misleading in many ways. As the example of Germany shows, what is at stake is not a mere matter of taste. Nor is it enough to leaven a large faculty with one or two Socratic teachers. We need many.

It does not follow that each should abandon his own field to become what poor polemicists occasionally call "a self-appointed critic of the age." As if this were a calling to which one could also be appointed by someone else! In any case a Socratic teacher does not sit in judgment on a throne above the contest. The Socratic ethos is to probe and question. And it would be well if some of those appointed to professorships felt that it was part of their job to do this, each in his own field.

In whose field are values, faiths, moral codes, and ideologies? If they did not lean over backwards to eschew Socrates' heritage, professors of philosophy and religion, literature and art, history as well as politics and economics, sociology and anthropology, would surely find themselves confronted with such topics in their own fields. Without taking time out to master computers or gain some other newly fashionable expertise, they could explore with their students some especially compelling alternatives to current fashions. In the process they might ask how various orthodoxies of our time look from the outside, how well grounded our common sense and all sorts of scholastic as well as nonacademic consensuses are, and what might be said for and against each alternative.

To be exhaustive is, of course, impossible, but students could be trained in the examination of a few particularly interesting and important alternatives. They could also be taught to look for alternatives. They could be imbued with a Socratic ethos.

Socratic teachers do not have to be visionaries. They do not need to develop views of their own. Teaching social philosophy, for example, a Socratic teacher might begin by having the students read Dostoevsky's "Grand Inquisitor," then Tolstoy's *My Religion,* T. S. Eliot's *The Idea of a Christian Society,* and Milton's *Areopagitica.* The students would be confronted with powerful and eloquent statements of radically divergent views. They would be free, of course, to agree with any of the authors read but would soon discover that they could not very well agree with many of them. They would be led to question the views presented to them—as well as their own views and the common sense of their parents, their friends, their society.

Teaching comparative religion or the history of philosophy, a Socratic teacher might exert himself to bring to life each view—each vision—that is studied, lending it his own voice, and confront the students with a series of challenges.

The Socratic ethos is critical, but in many courses it would be implemented best by teachers who excel at sympathetic understanding. Precisely those lacking a powerful vision of their own that requires detailed development might find a sense of fulfillment in bringing to life the visions of others. But the point would not be purely histrionic or aesthetic. The central motive would be to question our orthodoxies and the students' views now from this point of view and now from that—and to question each of these alternative points of view from the others. A strenuous task? Yes. A rewarding and exciting one that the students would both enjoy and profit from? Yes. A task for which one needs to be a visionary? No. A task that one could *learn* to perform? Yes.

By way of contrast, a scholastic teacher who was a Thomist might assign selections from the writings of St. Thomas, supplemented by some Maritain and some contemporary Thomists. A Marxist might assign selections from Karl Marx and Friedrich Engels, Lenin, and some contemporary Marxists. An analytical philosopher might look for an anthology or two of recent articles by analytical philosophers. In a seminar a scholastic might choose parts of one major work and supplement that with some recent articles discussing it.

A journalistic teacher would choose readings that have been much in the news of late: *The Greening of America* (1970) perhaps in the early seventies, but certainly no longer in the mid-seventies. The issues, too, would be picked in accordance with current fashion.

Actually, a Socratic teacher might also choose a fashionable text, but only to show what was wrong with it. In fact, any text can be studied scholastically, Socratically, or journalistically. The scholastic will teach one approach and— deliberately or unwittingly—try to indoctrinate the students, if only regarding the right way of doing things. The journalist will be most concerned to be interesting, exciting, and up to date—and will leave the students with nothing much worth remembering. The Socratic teacher will stress the need for critical evaluation of alternatives and continued self-examination.

Each of the three types can be exciting or boring, and a great deal depends on a teacher's personality. Most teachers certainly teach their students very little, if anything, that is remembered ten years later, and some teachers are loved for little more than their enthusiasm. Some professors are frustrated actors, and a few of these teach literature and spend a fair amount of time reading parts of plays to their students, taking all the parts. It would serve no purpose to expand our typology to accommodate this type. Yet teachers of this kind may open the eyes of some of their students to Shakespeare or Molière, or even to plays or poetry in general.

15

Visionaries are not necessarily particularly good teachers. They often come to feel that they have no time for the views of others—especially views that they consider obviously inferior to their own—and when they do discuss rival positions their heart isn't in it. As long as their vision is maturing, they may be excellent at taking students along on their voyages of discovery. But once they have spelled out their own positions, they are frequently far less effective teachers than are younger men and women who have no positions to defend.

Those who have begun to spell out their vision in print are in a bind. To repeat in lectures what they have published seems bad because the students could read it more quickly by themselves. Assigning it makes the students feel that the professor is pushing his own views and not impartial enough. Assigning one's own views along with those of others forces one into a defensive position in which one has to show how one's own position is superior. Those who do not assign their own books but summarize some of the main points briefly in the lectures without giving a detailed defense seem dogmatic. And those who refrain from assigning or discussing what they have worked out in print are actually leaving out what they consider especially important—

assuming that this is why they wrote about it—and then the course becomes unbalanced. Some teachers conclude that one should stop teaching a subject as soon as one has published on it. The dilemma remains, for if that counsel were adopted generally most of the leading experts would not teach their specialties.

This multiple dilemma helps to explain why professors often become less popular as teachers after they win international fame. This is certainly not an iron law, but there are conflicting pulls that favor teachers without visions of their own.

Of course, one could design an educational system that would make things easier for visionaries. Until well after World War II there was relatively little room for discussion in the German universities. German professors gave lectures, and the German word for lectures is *Vorlesungen,* which means readings. German professors read their works in progress to their students. This gave them an opportunity to present their vision, or what the philosophers called their system. The students had no opportunity to raise questions, nor were the lectures coordinated with discussions of reading assignments. This method of teaching would have been highly problematic even if most of the professors had been visionaries. It was thoroughly authoritarian and did not foster a critical spirit.

Moreover, even professors who did have a system were not necessarily visionaries. To quote from ''The Academic Zoo'' once more:

> Most birds soar through the ether, but
> since peacocks cannot fly they strut.

When the Nazis came to power in 1933, a student who later emigrated to the United States and became a famous philosopher was writing his doctoral dissertation in Berlin under the supervision of a Jewish professor who decided to accept a call to the University of Istanbul. The student had to ask another professor at the University of Berlin to serve as one of his examiners. Herr Geheimrat Professor Dr. Maier has no claim to fame except for his role in this story. Before the student could be examined by the Herr Geheimrat, he had to master "Herr Geheimrat's system." Since this could not be done quickly by way of the lectures, the student took private lessons with one of Herr Geheimrat's assistants. Whenever he asked her a question, she would answer: "In Herr Geheimrat's system everything meshes with everything, and you cannot understand any part until you understand the whole." When the student finally was ready to take his exam, Herr Geheimrat did precisely what he would have done if Kierkegaard had invented the whole story. He died. And his system died with him.

The Socratic ethos stands opposed to this sort of vanity, but it may be thought to foster relativism. In fact, it does not. It nurtures a critical spirit and immunizes students against the facile notion that any view is as good, or bad, as any other. Students are taught to distinguish clearly untenable views from the few positions that appear to be defensible.

Socrates' heirs reject relativism no less than dogmatism; they aim to show how most views are untenable. But they are not committed to refuting all views or to finding all they reject equally bad. Some solutions of a problem are more confused and inconsistent than others; some are only slightly flawed; and one, or perhaps two or three, may be acceptable. It is worth remembering that Socrates had standards for which he was quite willing to die, and he was far from supposing that any norm or argument or book is every bit as good as any other.

The students of a Socratic teacher will realize that he is neither a relativist nor a dogmatist, and that he does not consider it his mission in life to teach them "the Truth."

Instead they learn to avoid all sorts of mistakes, and a Socratic teacher should be able to quote the words of Socrates at the end of Plato's *Theaetetus:*

> If you should ever conceive again . . . your budding thoughts should be better as a result of this scrutiny; but if you remain barren, you will be gentler and kinder to your companions, having the good sense not to fancy that you know what you do not know. . . .

Why, then, has the Socratic teacher become a rarity? One might suppose that scholastics would appreciate the Socratic rigor. They do—as long as it stops short of their consensus, their know-how and know-what.

This should not surprise us, and yet it is strange when one recalls how during the first half of the twentieth century "Socratic" was a term of praise for teachers, especially in the United States, and Socrates' hyperbolic claim that "the unexamined life is not worth living" was one of the most popular slogans in the academic world. What happened?

16

In the United States the turning point coincided with the McCarthy period after World War II when it became politically unsafe to question the consensus. It became ever safer to become increasingly scholastic. Sad to say, most academics are timid conformists. Many go into teaching because schools provide a sheltered atmosphere and more security than is to be found anywhere else. Having finished school, they do not want to leave. If possible, this last point applied even more in the United Kingdom than in the United States. Yet the growth of scholasticism is worldwide, and this explanation is insufficient.

In the Communist world the Socratic ethos had no place in any case and was never tolerated in the universities. In the rest of the world the most crucial fact was that after World War II higher education was extended to far greater numbers of students than ever before. It ceased to be a privilege to which a few were entitled, and became highly competitive. Rather suddenly, masses of new teachers were needed, and in the process academia became infinitely more professional, scholastic, and anti-Socratic.

Students became more concerned about examinations, and professors about publications. Neither had much time left for Socratic questioning. It is no accident that Socrates did not prepare his students to take tests, and that he did not publish anything. It does not follow that one could not devise Socratic essay questions for examination, and books can certainly breathe a Socratic spirit. But it is easy to see why most tests were un-Socratic and based on a consensus, and why the masses of new teachers published scholastic articles.

Not being visionaries, they could not spell out in print a vision of their own. And since they did not see much, it is not surprising that so many of them took to writing lengthy papers on small points. The old German doctoral dissertation became the model for scholarly publications. It was supposed to be a contribution to knowledge, nothing Socratic. And since most teachers could not make any large contribution, microscopism grew by leaps and bounds.

This development is ubiquitous throughout academia. A few brief illustrations will show what we are up against.

In the 1950s most philosophy departments in the United States had two standard courses that were required of all philosophy majors and a boon to students interested in taking no more than a little philosophy. One dealt with ancient philosophy, the other with modern philosophy, from Descartes to Kant. Gradually, this sequence has disappeared at most colleges and universities. More and more professors came to feel that they lacked expert knowledge to cover so much ground; and the papers they must publish to obtain professional advancement could at most deal with a single problem in one book by one philosopher. Moreover, almost all philosophical journals came to prefer nonhistorical articles. Increasingly, people became more interested in the future than in the past. By 1970, anyone teaching a course that dealt with three or four philosophers was likely to be asked whether it would not be better to devote a whole course to one of them, and more specifically to one or at most two works by him. The historical courses still offered have become more and more unhistorical, and Socratic comparisons of different views together with the questioning of our present common sense has given way to ever more technical discussions of ever smaller points.

Once this development has gained momentum, the Socratic critic is experienced as a threat by the scholastics whose consensus he is calling into question. They feel much less menaced by scholastics of another school of thought, for the ethos of other scholastics is much more like their own.

What we encounter in other fields is very similar. In literature departments the so-called new criticism has had its day, but it served as the vanguard of a microscopic and anti-Socratic professional orientation. One ceased to care about poets or novelists as human beings, about their world views or their perhaps withering critiques of their society—or, by extension, ours—and instead of this one traced their imagery or details of their diction. Not to see the forest for the trees in it became a virtue, and the study of a single leaf came to be thought of as superior still.

In religion two examples from a single department may suffice. One professor had begun his career with a book on the relevance of the Hebrew prophets, but in the last years before his retirement he got grants for studies of weights and measures in the Bible. A younger colleague whose first book had dealt with Martin Buber and the I-Thou relationship turned to analysis of arguments about the old scholastic arguments for God's existence.

Of course, it does not follow that the early books were better than the later articles. There is a great deal to be said for careful craftsmanship. But the change of orientation remains striking.

One could multiply examples from all humanities departments. One could even say that they are doing their best to cease to be humanities. They have come to eschew the study of humanity and the critical examination of our values, faith, and moral notions.

Something important has been lost. It would be silly to claim that many people used to do superbly what hardly any do at all today. I am not trying to eulogize the dead past. The question is what we should attempt in the future.

17

It can hardly be denied that the prestige of the scholastics has grown enormously since World War II while that of the Socratic ethos has declined. Yet there is room for conflicting interpretations. Some observers would say that the humanities are dying, perhaps even that they are committing suicide. Others would insist that respectability depends on being scientific, or that progress does, and that the notion of humanities departments as an equal branch besides social science and natural science departments is antiquated. Either way the humanities would have no future.

The most relevant questions, however, are rarely asked. Diagnosticians have often operated with highly misleading categories, as if the question confronting a professor were whether he wished to be a prophet and thus a fraud or a hard-working professional who contributes to progress in his discipline by finding his models in the sciences. There is some presumption among scholastics that whatever is of interest to people outside one's specialty can hardly be respectable and must be journalistic. Being unable to follow the papers published by mathematicians, one tries to publish articles that will be almost equally incomprehensible to all but a few colleagues. One simply fails to ask what alternatives are available, what kind of progress has actually been made since World War II, whether Socrates' job needs doing, and who is to do it.

The typology offered here should permit a better diagnosis. In the sciences, too, there are a few visionaries and legions of scholastics. Humanities professors, disclaiming visionary and prophetic powers, have modeled themselves not on the great scientists—nor would it make much sense to try to be an Einstein or a Newton—but on scientific scholastics, with dubious success. In the process much of their work has become trivial. It is arguable that the work of most humanities professors has always been trivial, and that it is only the numbers of the teachers and the volume of their publications that have mushroomed. But what has increased no less is the presumption, the loss of self-perception, the delusions of grandeur about progress, about a revolution in philosophy, and about working on the frontiers of knowledge.

The agencies and the foundations that give grants to professors have for the most part swallowed this bombast. After all, they must rely on the expert advice of professors. Applicants for grants have long learned that a project that laymen can understand is not likely to be funded, any more than a paper that laymen could read is likely to be printed in a professional journal. The way to demonstrate one's competence is to be technical. By the time one has one's doctorate, all this is second nature. Again, the dissertation is the paradigm.

When one is asked what one is working on, it is embarrassing to give an answer to a colleague that would not have stood up when one was working on a doctor's thesis or that would not do when one applies for a foundation grant. A Socratic answer would be as ridiculous as a visionary reply. The thing to do is to mention something small and technical, and what makes the best impression is a topic so refined that the questioner could not possibly hope to understand it short of a lengthy explanation—and perhaps not even then.

Thus thousands of professors were thriving while the humanities were dying. Only in the late 1960s was there a brief revolt.

18

The revolt was led by students who noted the desiccation and dehumanization of the humanities and social sciences. They could hardly be blamed for not grasping very well what had happened. Their demand for "relevance" was understandable, but their interpretation of that slogan was for the most part very crude and anti-intellectual. They spoke much of unmasking the establishment, but never succeeded because the fiendish conspiracy that they wished to expose did not exist. But without realizing it, they did unmask the conformism and timidity of many professors who, lacking any clear conception of their calling, aimed to please.

It would lead too far afield at this point to attempt any detailed analysis of the students' claims, the professors' reactions, and the changes made as a result. But one way in which a great many professors aimed to please ought to be mentioned. They became "relevant" in their spare time, orating about morals and politics without professional constraints, without professional rigor, without professional conscience. The point was to demonstrate a *social* conscience and to show that one's heart was in the right place— or rather on the left. But the conviction that the realm of faith, morals, and politics was the domain of passion and emotion was not questioned, and many scholastics saw nothing wrong in principle with the students' inference that the best way to demonstrate the depth of one's emotion and to bring about results was to use force.

It would have been a miracle if the changes brought about in this way had happened to be wise. It is no wonder that so many of them were extremely ill considered. Understandably, there was a protest against excessive emphasis on examinations and on publications. The result in many places was a drastic lowering of standards and a further decline of the humanities. In some universities in Europe faculty ranks were swelled with young mediocrities who, as was soon discovered, but too late to remedy the situation, left no openings for brilliant students. Elsewhere, from Berlin to Adelaide, faculty as well as students argued that political tests were more important for faculty appointments than academic qualifications. For the students a great many requirements were dropped, including not only a lot of examinations but also so-called distribution requirements that had formerly prevented at least extremes of specialization. In the wake of the revolts, specialization at the graduate level increased more than ever.

The more and more popular option of writing papers instead of taking examinations would make more sense if students were required to learn how to write. Most of them do not know how, and most of their teachers do not know how to write either, except articles for scholarly journals that are not meant to be comprehensible to anyone but a few colleagues with the same specialty.

To some extent the student revolutions were directed against some of the evils of scholasticism. But in the absence of any halfway adequate diagnosis of the situation— lacking the very concept of scholasticism, not to speak of the Socratic ethos—the rebels only made scholasticism worse.

19

The notion that the humanities are dying of desiccation and inanition may seem questionable. There is wide agreement—a consensus—that specialization is good and that only fellow specialists can judge the work being done. And scholastics are often very enthusiastic about the work of their peers and friends. Frogs approve of croaking.

It is idle to pit metaphors against each other or to debate the merits of what is being done. But it is important to note what is *not* being done.

Some scholastics are unquestionably very good at what they do, and if you ask other scholastics they will testify to that. But there are also many things that they either do not do or do badly; for example, three.

First, they do not cultivate Socrates' ethos. When they deal at all with faith and substantive moral and political questions, they usually do it after hours, often emotionally and usually irresponsibly. Owing to their two-world doctrine, they seem to have checked their reason and professional conscience at the gate before entering this realm.

Second, the scholastics generally lack the category of the You, of the human being who has dimensions (in Shylock's phrase). When they write about visionaries this usually leads to farcical misunderstandings. Typically, the scholastic has no sense of context, least of all the human context, from which sentences and concepts gain their meaning, nor do scholastics realize that the context precludes many meanings. Whether St. Thomas quotes Scripture or a modern scholastic analyzes a text by Kant or by some poet or perhaps a picture, the spectacle is basically the same. One deals with a helpless object that can be used and not with a You, a human document that confronts and challenges us. (This point will be developed in the next chapter.) It is exceedingly ironical that many scholastics took up the slogan of the student rebels who claimed that "the establishment'' had no respect for persons and dehumanized us, without realizing how they themselves were advancing this process and dehumanizing the humanities as well as their students.

Third, the scholastics generally lack perspective and fail to see *larger* contexts. Their lack of a historical sense and their inability to see the historical context of their own school and of its point of view are merely examples of this. Their attitude toward their specialty furnishes another crucial illustration.

At a conference on Machiavelli or on philosophy of language it is no longer startling to find that even top scholars who specialize in political theory or theory of knowledge and who have read and taught the basic materials cannot follow the lectures and discussions because they revolve around some recent articles that are never identified and summarized. This is no longer felt to be a lack of basic courtesy; it is widely considered an essential ingredient of professionalism. The scholastics fail to see how such practices facilitate an uncritical reliance on a narrow consensus. They disparage attempts to make things clear for those who do not share the same specialty, although such attempts are really invaluable because they force us to step back sufficiently to see the context of our specialty and to become aware of our assumptions. When trying to explain something to fellow scholars in another field, or to any intelligent and critical person, one generally learns a great deal. In their serious work, scholastics prefer to address only those who agree with them on essentials. As a result we are losing a whole dimension of discourse.

Some scholastics dabble in journalism after hours, writing things that can be understood by specialists in other fields and by educated laymen. But these excursions do not have the same importance either in their own eyes or in fact as their attempts to make contributions to their specialties.

Thus their writing in this vein is of a piece with the sophomoric notion that interdisciplinary courses should be relegated to the sophomore level, as if only highly specialized work could be serious.

In fact, many of the problems most important for humanity—including, as I hope to show in Chapter 6, punishment, dying, and medical ethics—demand an interdisciplinary approach. Those who deal with them only from the point of view of their specialty, whether that should be French literature, physiology, or linguistic philosophy, confine themselves to triviality. Those who really wish to work on the frontiers of knowledge must cross the frontiers of their departments.

20

Plato thought that there were only three basic types of mind and possibly a fourth that was not worth discussing—that of the slave. Nothing I have said is meant to suggest that there are only three basic types and possibly a fourth that is not worth discussing—that of the journalist. There are many more types, and a typology depends on a perspective, which is a point often overlooked. An employer looking for a good secretary would not find my typology very helpful.

My typology is based on a concern with higher education. Plato's was offered in a similar context, but his primary concern was with justice and the ideal city-state. He argued that both depended on the recognition of three human types that could not be changed by education. His types were, he thought, innate and hereditary, although now and then a rare child might not be of the same type as its parents. He considered it important to determine at an early age, but did not say precisely when, whether a child was essentially ordinary and fit only for training in a craft or business, or whether it had a strong enough spirited element for training as a soldier. Both boys and girls could have this, and a few of them—his third type—might also have such a strong reason that, after being trained as soldiers, they might eventually go on to learn mathematics and, after the age of thirty-five, philosophy. The teachers, he assumed, would all be of this third type, and differences among them were of no concern to him. There is no evidence that he ever noticed that he himself was very different from Socrates, or that the teachers turned out by his system of education would be very unlike both. His psychology was very crude.

My typology is not designed to classify children or applicants for college admissions, any more than soldiers, politicians, or neurotics. I have not yet discussed the conditions that might favor the development of visionaries, but it is worth noting that great visionaries have hardly ever been children of visionaries. Journalists are surely made and not born. I have commented on four types but concentrated on two, the scholastic and the Socratic. Neither of these two is innate or hereditary, and whether we get large numbers of either of these types depends on the education we offer.

Both types are encountered on the faculties of colleges and universities. Since World War II, higher education in most countries has produced unprecedented numbers of scholastics, and scholastic college teachers have increased by leaps and bounds while the percentage of Socratic teachers has decreased to the point where this type might become extinct. During the same period insufficient thought has been given to the questions whether this development is desirable and inevitable. I have tried to show in some detail that it is neither desirable nor inevitable.

One could expand this typology to make it more generally applicable. The term "visionary" could be retained, but instead of "scholastics" one might in that case speak of "technicians," and instead of the "Socratic type" one might after all speak of "critics," making it clear that what is meant is not the caste of professional reviewers. Then one could say that for certain jobs one needs technicians, while for some others it is desirable to find people with some vision, and for yet others those with a critical talent. Still, it would be pernicious, I think, to try to classify people along these lines before they embark on higher education and to push them into this channel or that. The point of my typology is not to make it easier to push people around but rather to make them aware of alternatives to enable them to choose this path or that with their eyes open.

Obviously, good technicians are preferable to bad critics. Yet André Gide had a point when he said in his journal for *The Counterfeiters:* "To disturb is my function. The public always prefers to be reassured. There are those whose job this is. There are only too many."

If most professors were like Gide, or if they were visionaries, our problems would be very different from what they are now. Anyone contemplating the future of the humanities today must start with the realization that scholasticism has become prevalent, and that for legions of professors their work is, in Einstein's phrase, a kind of "sport," if not a game, or a racket.

Perhaps another metaphor will prove more helpful. Most humanities professors are engaged in the analysis of a few chess moves, often moves by players who are not much better than *they* are. A few scholastics are very good at such analyses, and now and then one actually succeeds in discovering a new move.

For playing a whole game, life is felt to be too short. But it is arguable that life is too short to spend one's time analyzing a few chess moves or even to devote one's most creative hours to playing chess. If some people wish to spend their lives that way, let them be; but when this way of life is held up to generations of students as the best way of developing their talents, it is time to ask if this is not a death in life.

With all due respect for the finest players and the most brilliant analysts, the enterprises at which they excel are not the greatest of which human beings are capable. If these are the only role models that we present to our students, higher education ceases to be humanistic or humane.

The idea behind my typology is not to ring variations on the contrast between visionaries and technicians. My intent is even less to lament the dearth of visionaries. The point is more nearly to show how threadbare and pernicious this dualistic scheme is, and how the Socratic type represents a viable alternative. The scholastic notion that for young academics who are not great visionaries there is only one respectable alternative is wrong and harmful.

Of course, not every teacher is cut out to be another Socrates; but neither will everyone become another Bobby Fischer. If the highest peaks of excellence are out of our reach, we still have a choice between ideals. What we desperately need is more reflection on alternatives. For a long time we have bred mainly two types, the scholastic and the journalistic. The practical implications of all this need to be shown in the following chapters.

CHAPTER TWO:
THE ART
OF
READING

21

Reading is the core of the humanities and of the social sciences, but most students never learn to read well. Not even graduate students are required to reflect on different ways of reading. Yet professors and scholars read in some radically different ways—and most of them have never given much thought to alternatives.

Intelligent readers will not read Homer the way they read a newspaper, and one does not read encyclopedia articles the way one reads book reviews. In this chapter I shall concentrate on the reading of classics. I mean books or poems that are presumed to be worth reading more than once because they are considered inherently important and not merely sources of information about something else. Much of the material read in humanities courses is of this kind. It will be sufficient to distinguish four major approaches and a few subclasses.

The first approach is probably the oldest but still widespread today. The readers' attitude toward the author can be summed up briefly in the words: *We don't know and he does*. Such reverence goes back to times when texts were not plentiful and few people could read. The guardians of the scriptures impressed on their students that the texts contained some needful knowledge not available elsewhere. The origins of the scriptures were either shrouded in mystery or claimed to be divine. In places the meaning of the scriptures seemed plain enough, in other places extremely obscure. The many difficult passages lent credence to the guardians' claim that exegesis was required, and that they knew how to interpret texts while their students, to begin with, didn't. Typically, the exegetes first endowed the text with authority, then read their own ideas into it, and then got them back endowed with authority. This way of reading I call *exegetical*.

I use "exegetical" as a technical term in the sense just defined. All understanding involves interpretation, but not all reading is exegetical in this sense. We do not have to endow the texts we read with authoritv, nor need we read our own ideas into them. The exegetical reader does both.

The most obvious examples of this kind of reading are found among clergymen who read their thoughts for the week into scripture. This practice is not confined to one religion but found in Judaism no less than in Christianity, in Islam as well as Hinduism and Buddhism. Nor is it confined to minor figures. Martin Luther read *his* ideas into the Bible, and Albert Schweitzer *his*. Gandhi's reading of the Bhagavad-Gita furnishes another truly classical illustration. On the face of it, Krishna teaches a king who does not want to fight and kill that it is his duty to fight and kill, and in the course of his instruction he canonizes the caste system. Yet

Gandhi read into the Gita his own doctrine of nonviolence, and he lavished praise upon the Gita although he himself fought hard against the caste system. He found in the Gita only what he himself believed.

In the case of reformers who deal with a religious population, it may be argued that their own unsupported opinions would carry little weight and that, in order to be effective, they must read their ideas into scriptures. But neither Gandhi nor Luther was that cynical.

The case of Rabbi Akiba is instructive. In the late first and early second centuries of the Christian era he read his often strikingly humane ideas into the Torah, using exegetical devices that would have surprised Moses, as Akiba and his fellow rabbis admitted. But they believed that God had revealed to Moses or through Moses more than Moses himself had understood. What they discovered in the text, though often utterly implausible to anyone not trained in their peculiar form of exegesis, was held to be God's meaning.

We may thrill to Akiba's or Gandhi's humanity and concede that in their social and historical environment no other approach was so apt to convince those whom they wanted to convince. Still the fact remains that they read their own ideas into the text and got them back endowed with authority.

Essentially the same approach is common among scholastics, most obviously among the medieval schoolmen. Thomas Aquinas, for example, read not only scripture in this way but also Aristotle. Some modern scholastics read Kant in this way; and some who are not philosophers, Dante.

What is far stranger and has therefore not been widely noted is the recrudescence of this way of reading among existentialists. Kierkegaard, of course, was at heart a religious writer, but Sartre assured the world in "Existentialism

Is a Humanism'' that there were essentially two kinds of existentialism: Christian and atheist. He gratuitously claimed that Karl Jaspers was a Catholic and lumped him with Kierkegaard while calling Martin Heidegger and himself atheists. Actually, Jaspers had been brought up a Protestant and had become a kind of humanist, while Heidegger had been brought up a Catholic—and remained deeply Christian in many ways, not least in his way of reading.

Already in his book on Kant, Heidegger served notice that an interpreter must use "violence." His choice of this word shows how even before the Nazis came to power Heidegger was somehow charmed by violence. When they did come to power, he announced in his inaugural address as rector of the University of Freiburg that the time had come to kick academic freedom out of the university and for the faculty and students to add to military service and labor service the "knowledge service" of the Reich. This lecture, like Heidegger's subsequent appeals to the faculty and students to vote for Hitler, was published in 1933. Soon, however, he sought for authority elsewhere. His major publication during the thirties was a series of exegeses of some Hölderlin poems, eventually collected in a book. In time, he also published exegeses of poems by Rilke and Trakl, essays and lectures on the pre-Socratic philosophers, and finally two very bulky volumes on Nietzsche. His procedure was always the same: he endowed the texts with authority by casting aspersions on those who fail to recognize the greatness of the authors, and then he went on to read his own ideas into the texts.

Inspired by Heidegger, a whole movement developed in Germany that gave itself the name of hermeneutics, and many people abroad gained the impression that something new had been discovered. Heidegger himself seems to have felt that he had taught a generation how to read. But even as in his major work he resuscitated Christian ideas about original sin and the dread of death, he also brought back the religious way of reading on which he had been brought up—exegetical reading.

Sartre followed in the footsteps of Kierkegaard and Heidegger. In 1960 he announced in *Question de méthode,* which serves as a prologue to his *Critique de la raison dialectique,* that he considered Marxism "the philosophy of our time" and that it was impossible to transcend Marxism in our age—thus endowing Marxism with authority. And then he proceeded to read his own ideas into Marxism. Even as Kierkegaard could not accept the Christianity of the church of Denmark or any other established version of Christianity and developed his own subjective and by no means scholarly reading, Sartre could not accept the Marxism of the French Communist party nor that of the Soviet Union or any other establishment and he, too, developed his own subjective and by no means scholarly reading of a doctrine whose authority he posited at the outset.

There would be no point here in making so much of two or three individuals if it were not for the fact that they illustrate so well how a way of reading that one might associate primarily with rabbis, priests, and parsons is actually quite common among twentieth-century secularists. Many admirers of Marx are also very much like religious believers. They have not become Marxists by way of a thorough study of Marx and of rival thinkers whom they gradually discover to be inferior to him. On the contrary, they are Marxists first, and it is emotionally important for them to belong to this tradition. The study of Marx comes afterward and is usually no more scholarly in nature than was Kierkegaard's study of Christianity.

Kierkegaard openly spurned the scholarly approach and made a point of the fact that for his purposes there was no need to read the Bible in the original. Philological carefulness was beside the point. Heidegger's exegeses are almost always of German or Greek texts; German was his mother tongue, and he made a great show of his knowledge of Greek; but specialists find his readings unacceptable and often get upset about his untenable interpretations until they discover that they tell us much more about Heidegger than about the texts.

This is not a mere oddity about Heidegger, Sartre, or Kierkegaard. The exegetical approach is even much more common in literature departments than it is among philosophers. After all, a philosopher who disagrees with Hegel or Nietzsche has the obvious option of presenting his own views under his own name. A professor of English or French is much more apt to feel that he would go beyond his competence if he wrote a philosophical essay or book, and hence his philosophizing typically takes the form of exegetical reading.

22

Considering that highly intelligent people have been doing this for centuries, it may seem that this is perhaps the best way to read texts, and especially religious texts. Yet this approach is open to several crucial objections.

First, it almost always involves self-deception. The exegetical reader scarcely ever realizes that after endowing the text with authority he reads his own ideas into it and then gets them back endowed with authority. Even Heidegger, who openly spoke of using violence, went on to suppose that there had been some mysterious disclosure. Typically, it is assumed that something has been revealed when in fact one has closed oneself to any genuine encounter with another voice.

The exegetical reader does not even ask what the author of the text might have thought of this way of reading and of the exegete's way of thinking and mode of being. Any such challenge is forestalled. Yet the pre-Socratics, for example, broke new ground with their deliberate refusal to read exegetically. They never endowed Homer or Hesiod with authority, nor did they read their own ideas into ancient poetry. On the contrary, some of them spoke scathingly of the great poets; they were very critical of each other; and they refused to concede authority to any text whatever. It was by virtue of this epoch-making attitude that they became the founders of Western philosophy. Heidegger failed to see what was distinctive about them, read them as he was brought up to read scripture, and never thought of asking what these writers—or any of the others whom he interpreted at length—might have thought of him. In his reading there is no You. He always soliloquized.

This is typical of most ways of reading. An analytical philosopher once posed the question: Whom among the great philosophers would you choose as your companion if you had to spend a long time on an island with just one other person, it being understood that you could not discuss philosophy? Several other philosophers joined in the game, debating the relative merits of Kant and Marx, assuming all along that there was only one material question: What do I think of him? It never occurred to any of them to ask: What might he think of me?

This incident is also instructive in another way. It was assumed by all that philosophy is one subject among many others, and that one could easily agree not to discuss it. Many people will find nothing odd about that. But suppose you could choose as your companion Sigmund Freud, it being understood that you must not discuss psychology. Freud might have been a wonderful companion, and he had many interests, including literature, art, and religion. But the idea of discussing these with him without ever touching on psychology *is* odd because he brought to bear on everything his own distinctive psychological approach. Would something like this not be true of Plato and Nietzsche as well? Or would the analytical philosopher who posed the question say that some of their works as well as Spinoza's *Theological-Political Treatise* and Aristotle's *Poetics* were not philosophy? Thus the little game, which is likely to enliven any academic dinner party, throws some light on the professionalism of the scholastics. Philosophy has become something one can "do" from nine to five and that one can also choose not to do, for example, on vacations. A visionary or Socratic philosopher might have some difficulty understanding that. But let us return to the point that most readers, and by no means only philosophers, ask themselves only what they think of the author and never what the author might have thought of them.

The exegetical reader does not risk himself. He plays it safe and avoids *culture shock*. This is one of the most crucial objections to this approach; and culture shock is one of the leitmotifs of my argument.

A traveler who immerses himself in another culture, trying to see the world, including himself and his own culture, from an altogether different point of view, is likely to find this a very unsettling experience; and anthropologists call this experience culture shock. Few travelers, of course, immerse themselves as deeply in a foreign culture as do anthropologists who settle down in it to live there for a couple of years. Still, even a traveler who stays only for a few weeks can make a concentrated effort to discover what is distinctive in another culture, what is different from his own, and how his own culture, his habits, his ways of thinking, acting, and feeling might look to people in this foreign culture. Few travelers make a sustained effort of this sort. The exegetical reader is like an American traveler who, wherever he goes, stays at the Hilton, which is comfortable.

Finally, and this objection is as crucial as any, most exegetical interpretations are utterly arbitrary. This is not a dogmatic verdict that depends on a rival approach. Different exegetical readers come up with widely different readings of the same text and find each other's exegeses totally unacceptable. Nor is there any way of arbitrating between them. Hence they have often had recourse to killing each other— in wars when the numbers were large, by means of executions when the numbers were small. But even when this did not happen, Luther, for example, found the exegeses of the leading Catholic theologians and of Zwingli, his fellow reformer, wildly implausible, and they returned the compliment. This situation is closely paralleled among Marxists.

Among scholastics, of course, there is a consensus, and they do not read such utterly different ideas into the same texts—if they belong to the same school. Insofar as they share the same ideas, they read the same ideas into the texts. And insofar as they have lost sight of the existence of other schools, they are likely to deny that they are doing anything of the sort. But in addition to the several schools in medieval Catholicism, for example, there were also Jewish scholastics who read the Old Testament differently. And in the modern world there have been High Church and Low Church scholastics as well as a multitude of Protestant sects and the Orthodox church. Yet those who stay at the Hilton tend to suppose that everybody who is anybody stays at the Hilton, and that those who don't need not be taken seriously. They forget that the consensus which gives them a feeling of security is parochial. They studiously ignore alternatives. This keeps them from discovering that exegetical readings are always arbitrary.

23

If the first way of reading can be summed up in the words, we don't know and he does, the second can be summarized: *We know and he doesn't.* It is, in one word, *dogmatic.*

Obviously, the very same people who read some texts

exegetically are very apt to read other texts dogmatically. It should suffice here to distinguish three variants of the dogmatic approach.

The first finds expression in the refrain: *Had he known X, he would not have said what he did.* In this vein, a renowned Roman Catholic historian of philosophy has written a book on Kierkegaard in which he kept saying: Had he read St. Thomas, he would not have said what he did.

It would be easy to multiply illustrations by naming various Thomists or Marxists. Dogmatism of this type is so common that most readers should have little trouble supplying examples of their own.

This dogmatic approach to texts is rather like the kind of patriotism that proclaims that our country is the best. Even at one's most charitable one can hardly keep from asking: How do you know? In how many other countries have you lived? How many have you studied? And how much of an effort have you made to understand the claims of people elsewhere that their country is the best?

The second variant has a slightly different refrain: *Had he possessed our superior techniques, he would not have said what he did.* Occasionally, this claim, like that of the first variant, could actually be true. There may be passages in Plato's *Sophist* or *Parmenides,* for example, where he simply made mistakes. I should also concede that in studying philosophical texts it is important to examine the arguments of the philosophers closely. But it does not follow that the most distinctive views of Plato, Kant, Hegel, or Nietzsche were based on their arguments. If shown how one or another of their arguments was weak, inconclusive, or even outright fallacious, they might often have given up no more than that one argument.

The traveler who stays at the Hilton and merely looks out the window, or perhaps saw quite enough on his way from the airport, will never find it difficult to reassure himself that it really is not worth the trouble to venture very far afield. He will always find some things that are drastically wrong, and he can say, often with some plausibility: If they had our superior technology, they would not do things that way. This is a good way of avoiding culture shock. But what is the point of traveling to exotic places and visiting truly different cultures if that is the game one is playing? And what is the point of reading Plato in this spirit?

The third variant has a somewhat more gracious refrain: *He wasn't altogether hopeless and at points came close to some of us*. This is how some Americans have read Heidegger, trying to show that in places he says what John Dewey or someone else has said better. Another example of this variant is furnished by a recent book on Nietzsche: Nietzsche was not entirely hopeless but in places came close to Ludwig Wittgenstein and one or another Oxford don.

A generation earlier, Paul Elmer More had pictured the Buddha as a stammering Jesus who had great trouble expressing himself because what he wished to say could be said adequately only a few centuries later by Jesus Christ.

In all three variants, the dogmatic reader fails to ask what the author might have thought of this way of reading and of the reader's way of thinking, his outlook on life, his presuppositions. The dogmatic reader avoids self-exposure, blinds himself to alternatives and objections, and refuses to see what is distinctive in the text and could not just as well be found at home. At worst, his interpretations are arrogant and implausible; at best they are condescending and myopic.

24

The third way of reading texts may be summed up briefly as saying in effect: *We don't know and suspend judgment about truth*. I shall call this approach *agnostic*. Truth is out of the picture, and the reader's concern is with something else. Again it may be useful to distinguish three variants.

The first is *antiquarian* and flourished in the nineteenth century, but can be found in other centuries as well, including our own. One reads texts the way some people collect stamps, perhaps with a preference for what is old and rare.

The second variant is *aesthetic*. Kierkegaard, who used this term in a special sense, would have applied it to all three variants, but I am here using it to characterize an approach that is mainly concerned with beauty and style. One can read Kierkegaard or Plato this way, a poet or a novelist, a religious scripture or any text for that matter.

The third variant is *microscopic*. It is flourishing in the second half of the twentieth century. One no longer has breath enough to read a whole book several times to get a whole view, not to speak of a writer's *oeuvre*. One prefers to study one poem, one passage, or one argument. In this way the author is spirited away, the encounter with a challenging You is avoided, and one deals with small pieces that can be taken apart.

In all three variants, what mattered most to the author is likely to be ignored and in any case is not considered particularly relevant. Once again the reader reigns supreme and does not risk himself, his views, his preconceptions. Of course, this approach is not equally inadequate in all cases. It does become perverse when applied to writers whose central purpose was to challenge the reader, or to get at some important truth, or to develop a large view.

It is entirely possible and by no means unusual for the same reader to be exegetical, dogmatic, and agnostic in turn. He may read the Bible exegetically, the scriptures of some other religions dogmatically, Aristotle in an antiquarian spirit, Kierkegaard aesthetically, and some recent philosophers or poets microscopically.

The way students are taught to read is certainly eclectic.

But on the whole their scholastic teachers alternate among the three major ways considered here. What all three have in common is that *one reads without encountering a You and takes no chances of suffering culture shock*. Though written by men and women, *the texts are dehumanized and read in a parochial spirit*. Since reading is the heart of humanities courses, it follows that the humanities are becoming ever less humane. But how else can one read?

25

Another attitude toward an author one reads might be summed up like this: We don't know everything and he doesn't; but we have some intelligence and he does; and we shall try to transcend some errors by engaging in a common quest, confronting the voice of the text as a You. It seems useful to designate this fourth approach with a single word, comparable to exegetical, dogmatic, and agnostic. With some misgivings, I shall call it *dialectical*.

This term has a multitude of meanings. It has been associated with Zeno, Plato, and Aristotle, with Kant, Hegel, and Marx, as well as many others, and it is quite difficult to determine the significance of the term even in Hegel alone. The first point to be noted about my use of the term is that I obviously cannot mean all the things for which the term has been used by others. Second, the term is often used for various kinds of sophistry or sleight of hand. To dissociate my employment of this word as sharply as possible from this sort of thing, it may be best to give two grotesque examples of dialectic in the bad sense.

One asks: What is dialectic? Answer: Two people fall through a chimney, and one lands at the bottom dirty, the other clean. Which one washes?

Of course, the dirty one.

No, the clean one.

Why?

Because the dirty one sees that the other man is clean and hence assumes that he is, too; while the clean one, seeing the dirty one, assumes that he must be dirty, too. Now, let us try again. Two people fall through a chimney, and one lands at the bottom dirty, the other clean. Which one washes?

We have just been through this; the clean one.

Of course not, the dirty one.

But why?

Because he sees how the clean one looks at him and puts his hand to his own face, and so he realizes that he must be dirty. Now try again. Two people fall through a chimney, and one lands at the bottom dirty, the other clean. Which one washes?

We have just found out; the dirty one.

Nonsense, who ever heard of two men falling through a chimney, and one coming out dirty and the other clean?

That is dialectic.

Often dialectic is simply a fancy word used for a form of argument by which one can "prove" anything. It is essential to realize this and to strip the word of its charisma.

There is a story about a famous twentieth-century dialectician. He held forth on Hegel in a seminar, and eventually a student managed to be recognized and had the temerity to suggest that the professor, who had written a book on Hegel and another on "negative dialectic," was wrong about Hegel. A long argument ensued, but in the end the student was able to confront his teacher with a passage in Hegel's *Phenomenology* that expressly contradicted the professor's claim. The great expert on dialectic was not embarrassed at all but lectured the young man: "What is dialectical is precisely that the text contradicts the author's intention."

When I speak of a dialectical approach to texts, I mean nothing like this, nor anything very similar to what Plato or

Kant, Hegel or Marx, meant when using the term. Even as I have used the words "exegetical," "dogmatic," and "agnostic" as technical terms that I have tried to define clearly, I shall use the term "dialectical" strictly in the sense that I am about to spell out now. What I mean by it is no more and no less than this.

26

Dialectical reading is distinguished by the fusion of three crucial elements. The first of these elements I call *Socratic* because it harks back to Socrates' dissatisfaction with "the unexamined life." So far from trying to avoid culture shock, dialectical readers look for it. They enlist the aid of the text in an effort to examine their own life, faith, and values. They ask what the author might have thought of us and our current orthodoxies. The dialectical reader seeks vantage points outside the various consensuses by which he has been conditioned. The text is to help him to liberate himself. The text is an aid in autoemancipation.

Nevertheless, I do not call this way of reading Socratic rather than dialectical, for Socrates himself did not use texts in this way and did not teach his followers how to read. Moreover, this is only one of the three elements that mark the dialectical approach to texts.

Reading different authors is like traveling to different places. The dialectical reader subjects himself to *multiple* culture shock. He is not looking for an authority with whom he can agree but rather for alternative points of view that allow him to reflect critically on his own views. Reading in this way enables him to become conscious of his own preconceptions and of the prejudices of the groups to which he belongs.

As noted earlier in the discussion of the Socratic type of mind, one need not be a visionary to teach Socratically.

Those who wish to teach their students to read Socratically can be quite self-effacing. They will help their students to become aware of their own values and those of their society—and to question the lot. Such teachers will go out of their way to select texts that reflect sharply divergent points of view—not merely scholastic infighting over microscopic issues.

At this point dialectical reading has something in common with Hegel's dialectic. It seeks out macroscopic conflicts between basically different views. Instead of exploring mainly the arguments and counterarguments of members of the same movement or school who write in the same set of professional journals, disputing points so academic that only a specialist can see what is at stake, the dialectical reader pits against each other texts that reflect different world views, attitudes, and sensibilities. And he does not come to the texts prepared to agree with one and disagree with the others, or with the presumption that he already knows what is worth knowing and therefore can point out condescendingly where a text is wildly wrong and where it comes close to the truth. The dialectical reader embarks on a voyage of discovery, hoping to learn from a variety of encounters.

27

The second crucial element of dialectical reading I call *dialogical*. The text is treated as a You and allowed to question us, as we question the text. The term dialogical brings to mind Martin Buber, but his way of reading and his concept of dialogue were open to serious criticism and not exemplary to my mind. Therefore I call this way of reading dialectical and not dialogical.

Buber associated the I-Thou or I-You relationship and dialogue with ecstasy that could be achieved only in rare moments and could never last long. In line with this, his way of reading was generally highly subjective and impressionistic, and his interpretations of Hasidic texts involved a truly radical, if very beautiful, transformation of Hasidism. Indeed, Buber's *Tales of the Hasidim* are a triumph of exegetical reading at its rare best.

What I mean by the dialogical element is rather different, though my conception is indebted to Buber. We must allow ourselves to be addressed by the text, we must hearken for its distinctive voice, we must try to discern how it differs from all other voices. We must permit it to challenge, shock, and offend us.

It is a sin against the spirit—in fact, two sins: cowardice and idolatry—to shirk this shock and to make a present to the text of the best we have—our own views. The reader who does that ends up by worshiping his own precious handiwork. But Moses and the prophets, Jesus and Luther, Kierkegaard and Kant, the Buddha and the Gita, have something to say that wants to be heard and would scarcely have appreciated the generosity of those who favor them with their own views, thus doing away with the offense.

The point of harping on culture shock, challenge, and offense is that this way of reading is not authoritarian. One does not endow the text with authority, one is not committed to making it come out right, one is not predisposed to agree with it. One *is* committed to trying to hear and understand it, and one assumes that in all probability it will not agree with us and not be agreeable at every point. The dialectical reader allows himself to be questioned, but he also questions the text. Feeling offended or shocked, he tries to formulate his own prior position; he compares that with the position of the text; and this becomes the beginning of a dialogue between reader and text. In the course of this dialogue, the reader's previous point of view is transcended and his level of consciousness raised.

"Raising the level of consciousness" is a phrase we have come to associate with dogmatists who meant that they were raising the consciousness of others—or even of "the masses"—to their own enviable level. This presumption is profoundly undialectical. When I speak of raising the level of consciousness I am closer to Hegel's *Phenomenology* than are dogmatists of this stripe. I mean raising our own level of consciousness through deliberate exposure to alternatives—which can be done through reading, travel, listening to music and seeing paintings and sculptures, through film and theater, but not through authoritarian indoctrination in one point of view by a steady diet of didactic films and plays and books. I have in mind an expansion of consciousness, the liberation from parochialism and cultural conditioning, the freedom that is born when the awareness of a multitude of alternatives issues in the creation of new ways.

28

The third crucial element of dialectical reading is *historical-philosophical.* It is only the fusion of this element with the Socratic and dialogical elements that makes reading fully dialectical in my sense.

This third element is best understood in terms of three concentric circles. *We begin with the inner circle by reading one whole work,* trying to get a whole view of it. Even when details slow us down and at times become so puzzling that we stop to see whether microscopic examination affords us any help, our primary concern is not with what is minute but with the author's central problems. We ask, as scholastic microscopists rarely do, what the author was trying to accomplish in this work. Instead of using a half verse from Genesis to our purpose, like Thomas Aquinas and legions of theologians and clergymen, we ask what Genesis is all about, realizing, of course, that this question cannot be answered until one has read the book in its entirety a great many times, taking pains over innumerable details.

Instead of occupying ourselves mainly with obscure transitions from one concept to another in Hegel's *Science of Logic,* or from one stage to another in his *Phenomenology,* like so many commentators, teachers, and writers of articles, we ask, as most of them never do, what Hegel was trying to accomplish in these books.

In all such cases we rely initially on internal evidence, without going outside the text. But we also ask: What did the author actually do? And what did he think afterward that he had done? Often the concluding pages or the preface furnish clues. And—to anticipate—the answers to these questions are often invaluable for an understanding of the author's next work.

In the case of a philosophical work any serious reading must involve some evaluation of arguments, solutions, and insights. Such evaluations need not be dogmatic; they need not proceed from an unquestioned rival point of view. The initial criticism can be internal. Subsequent evaluations can proceed from a variety of points of view. The same applies to religious works. One can first see how a sentence, a passage, or a story functions in its context, and then one can view it from different vantage points. Similarly, a passage in the *Iliad* or in a play can first be studied in its context to see how it works there, and then one can also look at it comparatively, contrasting, for example, Euripides' handling of Agamemnon's preparations to sacrifice his daughter, Iphigenia, who does not know her father's intent, with Abraham proceeding to sacrifice Isaac.

All major religious scriptures and literary works, no less than the books of the great philosophers, also have what I call a philosophical dimension. If they have that and we miss it, we have been bad readers. What I mean is not necessarily as intellectual as "a view of the world," although that phrase is often appropriate. Perhaps the best way of putting this point is to say that many texts reflect a distinctive experience of life. The dialectical reader looks for that—first of all and most importantly in the text.

Students taught by the new critics and other microscopists were generally not taught to look for anything like this. Instead they concentrated on the poets' and later also the novelists' diction, on words or imagery—or in philosophy on a few arguments or on the meaning of various terms. The best and most sensitive among the new critics occasionally did say something about a writer's experience of life, almost in spite of themselves. But what matters here is how they taught their students to read.

The new critics made much of the autonomy of a poem or a book and taught their students not to look beyond it either to the author's other works or to his life or letters. The philosophical dimension was ignored even in works where its importance could scarcely be missed, as in Sophocles' *Antigone*.

The new critics stressed painstaking respect for the text, the whole text, and nothing but the text. In at least two ways they did rather better than a great many analytical philosophers. First, their focus on the work as a whole compared very favorably with the ways in which analytical philosophers frequently concentrated on far smaller units while ignoring the context. Second, the new critics never tired of insisting how important it is to attend carefully to an author's language. In this way students were at least brought face to face with a distinctive sensibility.

Analytical philosophers have spoken of language quite as much as the new critics, and many also have the same bias against biography, development, and history. But their insensitivity to the language of the writers whom they studied, especially foreign writers, has at times been staggering.

This does not seem to have been noted widely and is therefore worth showing. I shall confine myself to some recent readings of Freud and Nietzsche.

The volume on Sigmund Freud (1971) in the prestigious "Modern Masters" series was contributed by a distinguished British analytical philosopher. In the bibliography one looks in vain for at least some indication that Freud did not write his works in English. It begins: "Anyone who sets out to write on Freud owes his primary debt to three important works. First, and most heavily, to the great *Standard Edition of The Complete Psychological Works....*" Only one non-English title is listed, and no translators are cited. The same philosopher has also edited "A Collection of Critical Essays" on Freud for another highly regarded series called "Modern Studies in Philosophy." Almost all of the contributors are well-known analytical philosophers—and appear to have read Freud in English without bothering to check the original texts. This is surely quite extraordinary.

After all, Freud was one of the greatest writers of our century, and he is extremely difficult to translate. Anyone who tries to translate no more than the quotations he needs in a scholarly discussion of Freud quickly finds how much is lost in the process. Moreover, Freud, more than anyone with the possible exception of Nietzsche, has taught us to attend to nuances, and it is odd that people writing seriously about him should feel no need whatsoever to do so. Finally, it used to be a matter of course that scholarly work, at least beginning with the dissertation, required recourse to the original texts, certainly in monographs devoted wholly to a foreign author.

Translating will be considered at some length in the next chapter, but insofar as it is a paradigm of interpreting, some preliminary comments are required here. It has come to be "felt" widely by undergraduates that any interpretation is as good as any other. One hopes that few professors would say that, but many have become incredibly latitudinarian. The best way to show briefly that many interpretations involve palpable mistakes is to mention a few crucial mistranslations which involve, and in turn prompt, serious misinterpretations.

At this point it seems best to turn from Freud to Nietzsche. That will allow me to deal very succinctly with points I have discussed in detail elsewhere. The only English version of *The Will to Power* before 1968 was done by a man whom the editor of Nietzsche's *Collected Works,* who knew the situation, called "the most gifted and conscientious of my collaborators." I might add that until 1950 *The Will to Power* was widely held to be Nietzsche's magnum opus, and Heidegger still propagated this view more recently. Yet, to give merely two examples of the quality of even the final revised version of this translation, Nietzsche's "cosmological" in section 12 was turned into "cosmopolitan"; and in section 86, where Nietzsche says, "Henrik Ibsen ist mir sehr deutlich geworden," which means, "Henrik Ibsen has become very clear to me," the old English version has: "In my opinion, Henrik Ibsen has become very German." The translator simply confused *deutlich* and *deutsch*.

That students often make such mistakes is common knowledge; that translations used widely by professors in the classroom and in scholarly books abound in similar errors is not so widely known. But most professors never make careful comparisons between competing translations before adopting one as a text, and many consider it obvious that "readability" should take precedence over accuracy.

One might suppose that poetry calls for the most careful attention to language. Yet many professors insist that what is most important is that translations of poetry should be "poetic." It is widely held that every generation must make new translations, rendering the classics into its own con-

temporary idiom, and that any deep concern with faithfulness to the original meaning is bound to make for poor and
unusable versions. Naturally, this leads to wildly untenable interpretations in the classroom.

Some scholars furnish their own mistranslations. To give
a striking example, *On the Genealogy of Morals* (1887) is,
without a doubt, one of Nietzsche's most important works.
It consists of three essays, and the second is entitled
" 'Guilt,' 'Bad Conscience,' and the Like.'' Nietzsche's
theory of the origin of the bad conscience is one of his major
contributions to moral psychology and remarkably similar
to the theory Freud developed in two late works in 1930 and
1933.

In 1965 a philosophy professor at one of the leading
American universities published a book, *Nietzsche as
Philosopher,* in which the bad conscience was converted
into "bad consciousness," although the German *Gewissen*
can mean only conscience and never consciousness.
The book was full of German words that the author had got
wrong, and those which recurred were misspelled consistently. The copious "quotations" from Nietzsche brought
to mind the undergraduate reporter and the passage about
journalists in Shaw, cited above in section 9. Anyone checking the nine indented quotations in a central section found
that every one of them was marred by serious mistranslations or unacknowledged omissions that ranged from a few
crucial words to as much as nine lines. But what was most
shocking was surely that nobody was shocked. What mattered to most of the professors who read the book was that
this was the volume that turned Nietzsche into a stammering
Oxonian—and thus made him accessible for analytical
philosophers. The lack of any concern for the You, for the
subject's distinctive voice and meaning, had become so
widespread that misreadings on this scale were not felt to be
serious.

This reaction was not by any means confined to analytical philosophers. Young scholars interested in German or in French philosophy expressed the view that this was an important book because it showed what needed to be done.

When accuracy and respect for the You are sacrificed in this way to "accessibility," it is journalism that triumphs. Comic strip versions of *Hamlet,* or of "Superman," provide the *reductio ad absurdum.*

Professors who write very badly may suppose that good writing is the mark of journalism. Yet most good writing is obviously not journalism, and most journalism is sloppily written. The dialectical reader enlists the aid of the classics to gain some perspective on his own time and to discover its ridiculous aspects. The journalistic reader does his best to make even Nietzsche timely and accessible, regardless of the fact that Nietzsche considered it a point of honor to be untimely and a critic of modernity.

As long as one speaks of respect for the You, culture shock, and gaining some perspective on one's time, one may seem to be less concerned with plain accuracy and careful scholarship than are scholastic interpreters. The point of these examples is to show how the opposite is the case.

Many scholastics have a journalistic ethos. Their reliance on consensus leads them to favor fashion and blinds them to what is unfashionable and a challenge to current trends and orthodoxies. Unwittingly, they become unscholarly.

Scholastics, of course, differ widely. For many of them the text is secondary, the author matters scarcely at all, and what counts is the game in which the text is a mere prop— rather like a board on which one tries to make some clever moves.

Analytical philosophy began as a protest against insufficiently high standards of intellectual integrity and has occasionally posed as having more or less discovered the intellectual conscience. Nietzsche sometimes made similar claims on his own behalf, although his distinctly visionary readings of some of his predecessors are obviously also open to criticism. Still it seems symbolic that most of his interpreters have found no place for his discussions of the intellectual conscience and of "bad reading." By shutting their eyes to this side of Nietzsche, they have had to come up with untenable interpretations of his thought.

Nietzsche and Freud are of special importance for the dialectical reader because, more than anyone before them, they called attention to the human being who finds expression in a text. That was the point of their enormous interest in nuances. In his short preface to *Twilight of the Idols* (1889) Nietzsche called himself "one who has ears even behind his ears, . . . an old psychologist." In 1948 Theodor Reik, one of Freud's disciples, called one of his books *Listening with the Third Ear*. Freud has gained the unwarranted reputation of having been "reductive" in a demeaning way, and Nietzsche's subtle psychology is still widely ignored.

The antipsychological bias of so many scholastics in the humanities is ultimately antihumanistic. They shut their eyes to the human realities that find expression in texts and in other human creations, and deal with their materials as if they were objects divorced from humanity. The way St. Thomas cited Aristotle is still paradigmatic, except that one does not always cite by way of agreement. What has remained typical is the striking disregard for context and for the human being behind the texts.

At this point, of course, we are still in the first circle, where we deal with one whole work. But a book, not to speak of a short poem, is not autonomous. We might as well stay with the *Genealogy of Morals* and note, first of all, that Nietzsche himself says in the preface that the book may well baffle readers who do not know his previous books. He assumes, he says, "that one has first read my earlier writings and has not spared some trouble in doing so." This did not keep the author of *Nietzsche as Philosopher* from informing *his* readers on the very first page of Chapter 1 that none of Nietzsche's books "presupposes an acquaintance with any other" and that one loses nothing by simply browsing in his writings.

A relatively trivial example may illustrate how it is necessary to move from the first circle to the second. Take the title of Nietzsche's book: *Zur Genealogie der Moral. Zur* is ambiguous and could mean either "Toward the" or "On the" Genealogy of Morals. Few readers of the original text would ever notice this problem, but a translator is an interpreter who has to read at least as carefully as any scholastic. In this case the problem cannot be solved as long as we confine ourselves to the book in which it arises. But *Zur* occurs often in the titles of the numbered sections of Nietzsche's so-called aphoristic books, and there it often cannot mean "toward" and always seems to mean "on." Hence the title must be rendered "On the Genealogy of Morals."

More interesting questions also make it necessary to transcend the inner circle. Was Nietzsche a nihilist? What was his view of truth? Did Kant believe in God? Was Euripides a "rationalist"? Nor can we be sure of understanding a Kafka story as long as we confine our attention solely to that story.

29

The second circle, which is larger than the first, *includes the writer's whole oeuvre and development.* But one may well ask why we should go on to that if our concern is with reading a text. There are essentially three reasons.

As we have just seen, sometimes the meaning of a word—and much more often that of a passage—cannot be determined as long as we confine our attention to one poem or book. Nor can we always be sure about the intent of a work until we also look at the writer's earlier works, and at times his later works offer important self-interpretations and self-criticism. While such self-interpretations cannot always be taken at face value, readers who simply ignore them on that account, assuming that they know far better than the author what he was about, display extraordinary arrogance.

Second, there is always the danger that we read our own concerns into the text. That we sometimes find our own concerns there is no proof of error, as a certain kinship to the author or having had similar experiences or intuitions may enable us to see what previous readers overlooked. But in every such case it is important to check whether we have not read into the text what was not there, and one of the best ways of doing this is to look at the writer's other works to see if they show similar concerns.

My claim, in *Tragedy and Philosophy,* that one of the central themes, though certainly not the only one, in *Oedipus Tyrannus* is the hero's concern with honesty, and the poet's conviction that exceptionally high standards of honesty, though admirable, are likely to plunge the person having them into unhappiness—and that Sophocles introduced this theme into a story of which it had not previously formed a part—is a case in point. This theme, like some others I found in this tragedy, was one of my own themes, and it therefore was imperative to ask if I had read it into a play I admired. At that point I found crucial confirmation in one of Sophocles' six other extant tragedies, his *Philoctetes.* Here the poet built his plot around Neoptolemus' high standards of honesty, which make for a tragic outcome that only divine interference could prevent; and again this had been no part of the story before Sophocles recast it. To make even surer, one must then go on to look at the rest of the writer's *oeuvre* to see how or whether this theme fits into the whole. What is crucial in the end is to obtain a picture of the author's *geistige Persönlichkeit*—his cast of mind or, in one word, his mentality.

When you ask scholars who are really at home in the works of some writer where he said this or that, they will sometimes say: "I don't believe he ever did say that." Or perhaps: "He could not have." Or at least: "He certainly would never have said it that way."

Suppose that you turn on the radio, hear Stravinsky, and ask someone else: "Which Mozart symphony is this?" Even one who has never heard this particular music before might well say without any hesitation whatsoever: "I don't know what it is, but it certainly is not Mozart." Similarly, one might say in the case of a painting by Egon Schiele: "I don't know whose work that is, but the notion that it could be a Giotto is simply grotesque." What is so obvious in the case of painting and music is not at all obvious to most readers of texts—which shows how badly most people read.

A critic who knows only one or two of Turner's more conventional canvases may feel sure when confronted with one of his impressionistic masterpieces that it could not be a Turner. One needs some awareness, if not intimate knowledge, of the whole *oeuvre* and development to gain some feeling for an artist's or author's spiritual personality. The better you know him, the greater is your power of discrimination.

Among art historians this kind of discrimination is often cultivated to a high degree, and experts will not hesitate to say of a "Rembrandt" in a museum: "The attribution to Rembrandt is certainly wrong." Or: "The face cannot have been painted by Rembrandt." Or: "Certainly an eighteenth-century imitation." The main reason why this kind of skill is so much more widespread in the case of music is surely that, thanks to radio and phonograph, many more people have heard a vast amount of music than have ever had the opportunity to see a comparable number of paintings. A great many people have heard most of the greatest works of Beethoven and other masters many times over; very few have seen most of Rembrandt's best paintings, and many that one has seen one has seen only once, briefly.

Texts can be studied quite as easily as music. Here the widespread lack of any skill in recognizing differences in style is due mainly to poor teaching. A dialectical reader will try to develop some sense not only of whether an author could have *said* certain things but also of whether he could have *meant* certain things. The suggestion that a writer he knows well should have meant *this* may seem quite as ridiculous to him as the notion that Mozart could have written *that* will seem to many others.

In music and painting we speak of style, we recognize that style has something to do with a period, and we operate, in effect, with the category of anachronism. We can often say with assurance that something is not only not Mozart but also cannot be eighteenth century. Exactly the same applies to paintings and to literary style. But there is also a style of thought that, like style in music or painting, points to one period and definitely precludes another; and a dialectical reader will look for a writer's style of thought and develop a sense for that no less than for his literary style.

Those who take pains to avoid culture shock and shut their eyes to what is distinctive in an author naturally do not develop any sense for his style and mentality. When they nevertheless write books about some past philosopher, their interpretations are often as anachronistic as would be books about Mozart or Giotto that ascribed to them works actually produced in the latter half of the twentieth century. Yet this sort of thing is so widespread that it is not greeted with the ridicule and contempt that would be showered on parallel efforts by interpreters of Giotto or Mozart.

Books about philosophers, and even more so courses

about philosophers, abound in grotesque examples. The way *literature* is taught, at least in translation, is frequently no better. The translations widely used in college courses give the game away. Often the accent is on freedom, and it is considered more important by far to have a version that is felt to be good poetry by current standards, which change rapidly, than a text that is faithful to the author's style and meaning. In this manner the most blatant anachronisms are not only tolerated but demanded, and any sense for the writer's style and mentality is ruled out from the start.

The notion that a Greek or German poet's work must first of all be recast in some contemporary idiom, and that it does not matter if in the process his images, his diction, and his meaning are changed, is comparable to the demand that before teaching Giotto we must commission a contemporary painter to produce copies in a currently fashionable style—Dali's in one decade, Picasso's in another, and then perhaps Roy Lichtenstein's—and base our instruction on these copies. When it comes to reading, many professors do not consider similar demands and practices grotesque.

30

One task remains to be accomplished in the second circle, which encompasses a writer's *oeuvre*. We must determine the weight of each text. We must find out, if that is possible, where it belongs in the author's development, whether he himself published it—and if so in what form, and what importance he attached to it—and if not, why not, and how authentic it is. Is it a passage scribbled on a scrap of paper that the writer himself would never have considered publishing? Or perhaps a fragment that he did not finish because he changed his mind? Or a draft superseded by a later version that the author did include in one of his books? Or is it something he himself did not write but that some student thought he had said in a lecture? If so, how likely is it that the student understood him correctly? And is the form in which the passage has been published and the context in which it appears perhaps misleading? These are merely some of the obvious questions one has to ask—and that rarely get asked.

Most studies of Hegel and Nietzsche, for example, show no inkling of such problems. To say nothing of lesser interpreters, consider only Jaspers' large *Nietzsche* and Heidegger's two-volume *Nietzsche,* and in the case of Hegel most British studies. The philosophers' development is largely ignored along with the other questions mentioned here.

In the 1960s we witnessed a reaction that is no less extreme and may well make matters worse. We began to get vast "critical editions" of the "works" of Hegel and Nietzsche. Yet the works that these men wrote and published themselves were in no desperate need of new editions. What is new and therefore gets much more attention is the editing of what really are not "works" by these men at all but notes and drafts or students' lecture notes. The overall tendency is thus to direct disproportionate attention to the texts with the least weight which are, moreover, presented in a manner that virtually guarantees that none but a handful of specialists will ever read them through and gain at least some sense of the context. Much more often, volumes of this sort are bound to be browsed in by students and professors who will then go on to quote from them as if the snippets cited had the same weight as a passage in a finished book. And having consulted a new critical edition in this way creates a presumption of scholarship.

31

Proceeding from the inner circle of a whole work to the second circle of a writer's whole *oeuvre* and development is not enough. The dialectical reader has to transcend the second circle, too, and consider it in the context of *the writer's background and influence*.

The historical background is crucial in at least two ways. Often it is impossible to determine the *meaning* of the text apart from this, and it is always impossible to determine the *significance* of the text as long as we ignore the background.

To be sure about the *meaning* of various words, phrases, and concepts, we often have to know the writer's predecessors. This is a commonplace in the case of ancient Greek or Hebrew. One consults dictionaries that list all the major occurrences of interesting terms—and in the case of words that are at all rare, all occurrences. In the case of modern languages, the literature is so large that dictionaries often fail us; but a scholar still has to move into the third circle.

Again a simple example from Nietzsche may illustrate the point. He called one of his last and most important works *Der Antichrist*. This has almost always been taken to mean "The Antichrist," but two extremely gentle admirers of Nietzsche have suggested that it really means "The Antichristian." Both renderings are possible; neither involves an obvious mistake. But the better one knows the second circle, the plainer it seems that Nietzsche at this point meant to be as provocative as possible. If possible, however, we find even more conclusive confirmation in the third circle.

Section 109 of the second volume of Schopenhauer's *Parerga und Paralipomena* (1851) begins: "That the world has a physical but not a moral meaning is the greatest, the most pernicious, the fundamental error, the real *perversity* of mind, and is probably at bottom also what faith has personified as the Antichrist." In the brilliant preface which Nietzsche wrote in 1886 for the second edition of *The Birth of Tragedy* he claimed that in this work "that 'perversity of mind' gains speech and formulation against which Schopenhauer never wearied of hurling in advance his most irate curses. . . .'' In other words, he suggested that he was, so to speak, the Antichrist. He was also aware of Ernest Renan's *L'Antéchrist* (1873).

In this case the third circle helps us to determine the meaning of a word. Much more often, we have to move into the third circle to determine the significance of a passage. Without knowing the historical background, we often cannot be sure whether the text is original or a pastiche, a parody perhaps or a polemic, blasphemous or pious. As long as we do not really care about the You and the intention of the text, all this may seem irrelevant. But if we do care about that, we cannot dispense with some knowledge of the historical background.

In the case of very influential texts, even dialectical readers will have to be extremely selective in taking *influence* into account. Otherwise they will never get anywhere because the material is too vast. Yet it will not do to take the easy way out and ignore this dimension altogether. If we pay no heed to what earlier readers have made of the text, our own reading is likely to be very narrow and subjective. Major readings of the past will make us aware of dimensions that we might otherwise have overlooked, and they may also help to keep us from reading our own concerns into the text. Hence some awareness of the range of the influence of a text and some explicit evaluation of a few prominent readings are essential. The dogmatist may be content to present his own view as the truth. The dialectical reader enters into a dialogue not only with the text but also with previous readers, commentators, and interpreters. Some of them help to protect us against pitfalls, if only because the errors of others are generally easier to recognize than one's own mistakes, while others show us problems and mistakes that without their help we might have overlooked.

The scholastic reader often pays attention only to interpretations offered by a few members of his own school, if that. He is apt to criticize the readings offered by some colleagues who in all essentials share his point of view, approach, and biases. The dialectical reader goes out of his way to see how the text has been interpreted in different periods by people approaching it in a variety of ways. That affords him a better chance of offering something more than simply one more reading.

32

It should be clear now why I call this way of reading dialectical. It owes something to Socrates, who was a dialectician in some sense, but it also goes beyond Socrates in its insistence upon treating the text as a You, looking for the experience of life that finds expression in the text, and taking into account the historical context. My approach also owes something to Buber's conception of dialogue, yet Buber hardly exemplified the approach advocated here. The historical-philosophical element owes something to Hegel, and yet Hegel, too, was not a dialectical reader in my sense. Nor is this approach eclectic, taking a little from here and a little from there. It has developed through a series of encounters—through dialogue with previous thinkers who can help us to avoid excessive one-sidedness. It has also developed through reflection on very different ways of reading, and the account given here is in places quite polemical. It may be more fashionable to avoid polemics of this sort by simply ignoring alternatives, but I have tried to show why this won't do. It is essential to consider alternatives and see what speaks for and against them, and what speaks for and against our own ideas. Dialectic always involves negations and polemics.

In this spirit it may be well to conclude by replying to a few objections that might be raised against the approach developed here. First, some readers will question the need for a historical approach to religious, philosophical, and literary texts. That is not a philosophical approach, they may say, or not a literary approach; that is history, and our concern is not with that. It is well to remember how much opposition there was to the historical approach to religious texts when that was developed in the nineteenth century. This opposition was born of the desire to protect the exegetical approach and to safeguard those who insisted on everywhere staying in the Hilton. They wanted to go on reading their own ideas into sacred texts in safety, without ever encountering challenges for which they were not ready. The case is no different nowadays in philosophy and literature.

Others may say: Who cares about history and the past, when our concern should be with the future? But I have tried to show that we need history to be sure about the meaning and significance of classical texts. And if we do not care what the author meant, why take his name in vain? In that case we might just as well stay home and play real chess.

Next, some readers might object to the concern with a philosophical dimension when it comes to texts that are not philosophical. I respond: Some philosophical texts lack what I call a philosophical dimension, but some non-philosophical texts have it; for example, Genesis and Job, Sophocles and the Dhammapada, Goethe, Tolstoy, and Rilke, and religious scriptures and Greek tragedy quite generally. Texts of this sort we simply do not understand adequately as long as we ignore the experience of life they express or their challenge to us.

Finally, it may be objected that the dialectical approach calls for too much interdisciplinary learning; that it is too difficult; that most students and professors simply lack the competence to read texts in this way. This is surely true. It ought to make for a certain amount of humility. The great philosophers were not ordinary people. Plato and Aristotle made all the knowledge then available in Athens their province. Descartes and Leibniz were as great as mathematicians as they were as philosophers. Spinoza was an encyclopedic philosopher, wrote a Hebrew grammar, and pioneered Biblical criticism. Hobbes translated Homer and Thucydides. Hume wrote a multivolume *History of England*. Kant advanced a major astronomical theory and, almost as much as Hegel after him, dealt with almost all the major fields of knowledge. Nietzsche, a classical philologist, was also the first great psychologist as well as a major poet.

In different ways, the Greek tragic poets and Dante, Goethe and Tolstoy, are no less awesome. Most professors clearly do not find the writings of such men congenial and can hardly hope to understand them well without a very concentrated effort that requires them to go beyond their specialties. That this is hard is obvious, but it stands to reason that reading Sophocles or Plato or the great religious scriptures would be hard.

No reform of education, especially in the humanities, can hope to get far if it does not pay attention to the ways in which students are taught to read. Not only are many great works spoiled for students in secondary schools by being taught so badly that the young lose their enthusiasm. When students and ex-students become enthusiastic about other texts a few years later, they are hampered by not knowing how to read.

In the 1960s large numbers of young people began to turn to the Gita, Zen stories, and other Asian texts, but simply had no idea how to distinguish between translations of widely different quality and between different interpretations (for the most part exegetical), nor did they know how to place the Gita or Zen in a historical context or how to inquire about the intentions of a text or its influence. If they had heard of "the genetic fallacy" or "the intentional fallacy," that did not help. They were groping in the dark, and this was largely because they had never been taught how to read classics.

Many professors who are very clever and extremely good at doing many other things have never thought of teaching their students how to read, and many of them have never mastered this art themselves. But neither television nor computers can save the humanities if the art of reading texts is lost.

CHAPTER THREE: THE POLITICS OF REVIEWING AND THE ETHICS OF TRANSLATING AND EDITING

33

So far I have concentrated on the reading of those texts which are the staples of most humanities departments. I have criticized the ways in which scholastics all too often read, and then have described an alternative way in some detail. I shall not deal at equal length with the reading of newspapers, scholarly articles, or materials one consults in search of some specific information. But it is worthwhile to dwell at least briefly on the reading of reviews which aim, or seem, to provide either a shortcut that makes it unnecessary to actually read books or some help in choosing what to read and finding what is most important.

Reviewers, translators, and editors are all middlemen who step between authors and readers. Having performed all three functions again and again, I do not mean this to sound disparaging. It is precisely because these functions play such influential roles that they need to be considered in discussions of the humanities. I shall deal with reviewing first, then with translating (on which I have already touched in the last chapter), and finally with editing.

Very little has been written about reviewing, although it is a prominent feature of our cultural life that meets the eye in newspapers and magazines, quarterlies and scholarly journals. Many people keep in touch with the world of books mainly, if not only, by reading reviews. Many professors write reviews, almost all rely to some extent on reviews written by others, and academic careers are also often influenced by reviews. When it comes to reappointments and invitations, salary raises and promotions, the reviews of a professor's books may make a difference. Why, then, has the subject rarely been discussed in print?

The answer is surely obvious. A great many reviews are subject, more or less, to Shaw's critique of journalism. One cannot discuss the subject seriously without going into this problem; but people evidently feel that this is impolitic. What would the reviewers say? Some of them would surely suggest that their critics are trying to make poor excuses for some bad reviews of their own previous work. As a result, the topic is rarely touched in print.

It stands to reason that anyone who has never published reviews would be ill advised to do an exposé, or at least would need considerable courage. But a writer who has contributed dozens of reviews to scholarly journals as well as weeklies, monthlies, and quarterlies really has no excuse for keeping silent.

Apart from the author and the reader, reviews involve two key figures: an editor and a reviewer. The editor's role is crucial. Editors decide whether a book is reviewed in their journal; who will review it; how long the review is to be;

when it will appear; and how prominently it will be displayed.

When the editors of many dailies and weeklies feature the same books while ignoring others, this does not prove that no decisions were made. The editors receive advance news releases and bound printer's proofs of the same books several months before publication, signifying that the publishers will make a special effort to promote these books, will advertise them and get them into many bookstores. Most bookstores order relatively few books in quantity. Not reviewing such books might give readers the impression that the editor was caught napping, while too many reviews of books that readers will have trouble finding in the stores would be out of place in journals with a wide circulation. Editors can take a chance on a few such titles that somebody persuades them to promote, but on the whole they have to think about what will be in the news and hence must pay attention to what will be advertised and written about elsewhere.

If that were all, few books that stand no chance of selling very well would be reviewed in daily newspapers and weeklies. But editors also feel some concern about what might endure, and they therefore listen to some experts. Few of these are visionary or Socratic.

A generation ago, *The New York Times Book Review* developed a brilliant system. Unable to judge with confidence which books should be reviewed, the editor decided to send out for review more books than he actually intended to review. If a review was unenthusiastic, it stood to reason that the book was not important enough to be reviewed right away; and if enough good reviews came in during the weeks ahead, the unenthusiastic review might never be printed. The reviewer got paid promptly in any case, though not much; but he was naturally disappointed when his labor turned out to have been for nothing. He learned quickly that if he wanted his material to be printed, it was better to be kind.

That is not to say that only good reviews were printed. In the case of books that were not likely to be in most of the stores anyway, a critical review seemed dispensable. But when a book is likely to be in the news, the matter is different. Often an editor can predict who would write an enthusiastic review of a particular book and who would probably try to tear it to shreds, and some editors would feel that they had failed in their responsibility if they gave a book by an author they admired to a hostile critic, or vice versa.

In the scholarly journals the situation is worse. Within the profession people tend to have strong opinions of one another, and editors should know who thinks what of whom. Thus it is often easy to obtain the kind of a review one wants, though editors, like other people, sometimes are surprised. Scholarly journals are often associated with a school of thought. When this is the case, it is not very risky to hazard a guess how a certain book will be reviewed.

Occasionally, editors print a review by someone who has never graced their pages previously and who seems to have been imported solely because he could be counted on to hate the book he is reviewing, or to rave about it. Most readers never seem to notice such things any more than the fact that some scholarly journals consistently ignore some authors whose stature far exceeds that of most writers whose every book is reviewed.

Since none of us has time to read most of the books of which we read reviews, and we have rarely read a book before reading reviews of it, most of us rarely notice how full of misrepresentations and outright errors ever so many reviews are. This is as true of favorable as of hostile reviews and also applies with full force to scholarly journals.

Plainly, most reviews should not be taken very seriously.

Some first-rate universities issue an annual booklet listing all of their professors' publications, except book reviews. While this suggests that the administration does not think much of reviews, it also serves to discourage those who would be best qualified to write responsible reviews and does its share to leave the field to the journalistic type.

With occasional exceptions, reviews are a form of journalism. But it may be useful to distinguish at least a few types of reviewers. There is, first, the professional reviewer. If he has to turn out several reviews a week, he must partially read a great many more books than that in order to make an intelligent selection, and he cannot be expected to read with great care all the books he reviews. He is admired, if at all, for calling people's attention to some books that might interest them, and whether everything he says about the books he discusses is right is considered less important.

Second, there is the famous scholar for whose reviews one looks. But most famous scholars consider reviewing a thankless task and prefer to get on with their own work. When they agree now and then to review a book because they feel that they will have to read it anyway, they often regret their decision after reading the book. To show up a book by a young or unknown writer seems cruel and may destroy his career. To show up a book by a professor who is a colleague at another institution is embarrassing if the book is full of palpable mistakes and no less excruciating if its badness cannot be demonstrated conclusively in a small space. Of course, a book may be good, but the trouble is that one often agrees to review a book, assuming that it will be good, and then it is not. Hence few great scholars write many reviews, and those who do write many generally spend very little time on them. Their most common strategy is to write a short essay on the subject of the book, using the review as an opportunity to advance their own views, and weaving in some remarks about a book—or often several books—that they have not read with any great care.

Third, there is the young reviewer who—to quote an apt phrase from Simone de Beauvoir's *Les Mandarins*—views the world from the height of an unwritten book. Reviews give him a chance to appear in print and show how clever he is.

Fourth, there are those who have written some books of their own without achieving recognition. Their own writing does not give them adequate satisfaction, and reviewing gives them a chance to get back at those who are more successful. Some people in this category are full of resentment; others derive such pleasure from their power that they gladly give good marks as well as bad. Some become "critics" and do not only feel superior to mere reviewers but argue in all seriousness that they are more important than writers because critics mold taste.

Finally, some people write short reviews, about one typed page per book, anonymously in some places, signed in others, sometimes with initials only. Some are encouraged by their anonymity to act irresponsibly or to be sloppy; others perform such a useful function in this genre that it seems a good idea to have prompt reports of this sort in a few competing publications about all books that have any claim to being serious. If these periodicals committed themselves to print prompt corrections of gross mistakes and misrepresentations, that might be one way of keeping them on their toes. Another would be to give the author an opportunity to add as much as one hundred and fifty words in the same issue, after reading the reviewer's copy. This might be an improvement on the German practice which allowed Hegel, for example, to publish a one-page description of his first book in a literary supplement.

Incidentally, one might suppose that the anonymity of reviews in the London *Times Literary Supplement* must have prompted gross abuses. Actually, the editor, realizing how easy it was for him to stack the cards, leaned over backwards to be fair. But in the seventies the tradition of anonymity was abandoned, and this seems better because reviews in the highly respected *T.L.S.* conferred an unmerited air of authority on reviewers who, though selected in good faith, were after all human beings with feet of clay; nor were all of them equally eminent. If a reviewer has no special expertise in the subject at issue, the reader should know that; and if the reviewer is a person of some eminence, then the review is understood more fully when it is seen as part of his *oeuvre,* in the context of his other writings.

Although some editors and reviewers have very high standards of integrity, it is certainly fortunate that reviewers of books do not wield the power of some drama and art critics. A few might like to be arbiters of taste, but their influence is very limited, especially since the advent of paperbacks. There are simply too many reviewers for any one of them to make very much difference, except for a piece now and then that manages to show conclusively how a scholarly book is in fact unscholarly.

Knowing how little their efforts matter in the long run, a few reviewers, like some film critics, aim at entertainment and write genuinely funny pieces that are thoroughly enjoyable for anyone who has not read the book, especially for those who have long disliked the author. Some weeklies maintain very high standards in this genre.

34

In the humanities one is, or ought to be, concerned with what endures. Engulfed by a flood of new books, one naturally wonders whether reviews might not be a guide of sorts to what will last. Yet journals, scholarly or not, give most of their review space to what is ephemeral; and they are better at dealing with mediocre books than at discerning what is more original and, in the long run, influential. To give examples from a few journals would be a waste of time, but the difficulty of recognizing what will endure can be illustrated by considering the Nobel prize for literature.

In some ways the work of the Swedish committee is easier than that of an editor or reviewer, for—to cite *Nobel: The Man and His Prizes,* edited by the Nobel Foundation (1962)—"Usually the literary awards have been given for an author's entire production" (pp. 82f.), and it seems less difficult to guess whether that will be remembered than to make a similar judgment on a single book the moment it appears. Moreover, the second annual prize went to Theodor Mommsen, in 1902, for his monumental *History of Rome,* making two very important points. First, literature was construed very widely, and second, as is duly pointed out in *Nobel,* the first three volumes of Mommsen's *History* had been completed in 1854–56, and the fourth in 1885. Thus the committee was confronted by an embarrassment of riches, especially during the early years, and one might suppose that it must have been relatively easy to give the first ten annual prizes to writers whose work would endure. Yet the praiseworthy awards to Mommsen, to Rudyard Kipling (1907), and perhaps also to Selma Lagerlöf (1909), stand out as exceptions.

In 1899 both Tolstoy and Ibsen had crowned their life's work with a masterpiece; but the first prize, in 1901, went to Sully Prudhomme. Ibsen died in 1906 and Tolstoy in 1910, and both were passed over annually. Rilke was perhaps the greatest poet of the twentieth century and published two of his best volumes in 1907 and 1908. He did not die until 1926, but never won the prize any more than Freud or Kafka. In retrospect it may seem baffling that these men were not considered safer choices than Björnson (Ibsen's compatriot), Mistral, Echegaray, Sienkiewicz, Carducci, Eucken (a German philosopher whose reputation, in spite of the prize, sank without a ripple), and Paul Heyse, of whom the chairman of the prize committee said in 1910 that "Germany has not had a greater literary genius since Goethe." All of these writers won the prize during the first decade. Tolstoy, Ibsen, and Freud were too controversial, being uncompromising critics of the faith and morals of their time. The chairman of the committee explained at some length how Tolstoy "has denounced the right of a government to enforce laws against criminals," and "though completely inexperienced in Biblical criticism, he has arbitrarily rewritten the New Testament in a half-rationalistic, half-mystical spirit" (p. 92). The nomination of Émile Zola, the author of *Germinal* and *J'accuse,* was felt to be a provocation because he was lacking in the requisite idealism and humanitarianism, being "the standard-bearer of the crudest kind of naturalism and could, therefore, not be considered" (p. 91).

It is arguable that the judgment of the committee has improved greatly in recent years, but our own judgment is less reliable as we come closer to our own time. In any case, the point is not at all that a committee in Sweden might have done better but only that it is far more difficult than we usually realize to recognize what will endure. Although a good education in the humanities ought to facilitate such judgments, it is no wonder that journals, scholarly or not, have such a poor record in this regard. They are really no better and no worse than one could expect from scholastics and journalists.

Of course, some editors try very hard to transcend cliquishness, some reviewers have extremely high standards of honesty even when they write reviews, and an occasional review is not only much better than the book with which it deals but worth reprinting. But not enough readers realize how many reviewers are returning or hoping for favors, or settling personal scores, or pulling their punches because it would be impolitic to be forthright. They do not wish to make enemies of certain people but can be sure of making friends by attacking others. An author who in a public debate wipes the floor with his opponent stands at least an even chance of soon being reviewed by him. In some countries all this is a well-kept secret, and as long as the reviewer and reviewee are not actually in the same department at the same university, the closest professional associations are simply overlooked, even when a book by one of the editors of a journal is reviewed by several of his coeditors in other journals, or when the chairman of a department reviews a book by a member of his advisory committee. In France all this is widely taken for granted, and people are cynical about it. It would be less than gracious for a French writer not to ask a friend who has written a book: What would you like me to say about it?

Many people fancy that they have mastered the art of reading reviews. But most of them merely discount reviews by those who do not belong to their own school while trusting reviewers who do. Those who are more sophisticated think that after reading several reviews they have a pretty clear picture of a book; and so they do; but no matter how clear it is, it may still be a caricature. The ancient Roman adage that a slanderer can count on it that *semper aliquid haeret,* something always sticks, is unfortunately true, and doubly true of what fits in with our prejudices. When we check our impression by reading a second review, we are apt to feel virtuous and well informed, and after reading three one feels that one is an expert on a book one has not read. We all know the remedy, which is to read the book; and we can do that, but reading reviews saves so much time.

35

Translations are another matter. Most of us do not rely on them unless we have to; but anyone with wide interests often has to. In the very early nineteenth century it was still possible for rare individuals to read most of the greatest Western works of literature, philosophy, history, and science in the original languages, as Hegel, for example, did. But even he did not know Hebrew; and Chinese and Arabic, Sanskrit and Pali, were outside the horizon of Western education. Today most students are at the mercy of translators, and more and more scholars depend on them, too. Nevertheless, few people have ever reflected on the ethics of translation.

Translators should ask themselves first of all about the purpose of their enterprise. If the aim is merely to produce a version that is easy to read and designed to make as much money as possible for the publisher, it is implicitly assumed that the translator's responsibility is solely to the publisher and not at all to the author or the readers of the book.

A very high percentage of translations, however, are designed mainly for use in schools. They are meant to be studied by students who will discuss, write, and be examined about the original authors on the basis of these versions. The courses are advertised as dealing with Buddhism, Homer, or Lao-tze, and that is what the students want to know about and, having done the work, will talk about. One might wish that at least their teachers were able to read the originals, but professors with wide interests are also relying on translations, even in some of their publications.

The moral implications of this situation seem obvious but have been widely ignored. Any translation that is meant to be used by students should be designed to serve as a basis for discussions of the original work. It should try to capture the author's tone, his meaning, and his distinctive voice. The translator's primary duty is to make the author's voice heard across the language barrier. He serves the writer ill if he turns a brilliant style into a dull and tedious medium, or if he makes the author say what he did not say. And he misleads the reader if he turns a difficult writer, like Faulkner, or an enigmatic work, like *Finnegans Wake,* into easy, flat, journalistic prose that can be read like a newspaper.

His publisher may press him to be clear and idiomatic, in a style that presents no difficulties; and some critics and professors may tell him that great books have to be translated again and again because every generation needs its own version—and that today poetry has to be done into Victorian verse, or into T. S. Eliot's idiom, or into what is fashionable *now*. But the translator who accepts advice of this kind betrays the author no less than his readers. The author's and reader's interests are essentially the same. The author has to be brought to life as a You who was different from other writers, and Sophocles should come out sounding like Sophocles, and Rilke like Rilke.

If every generation really needed a contemporary version of Homer and Sophocles, why not of Shakespeare? In the mid-seventies this need was perceived belatedly, and an American publisher issued *Macbeth, Hamlet, King Lear,* and *Julius Caesar* with modern paraphrases on facing pages. "To be or not to be; that is what really matters." And "Tomorrow follows tomorrow, and is followed by tomorrow." It remains for another publisher to discover that these translations are too faithful and wooden, and that we really need a version that is as poetic and free as some recent versions of Homer. Isn't "To be or not to be" rather prosy and abstract? How about "The choice between continued life and suicide, that is the really hard question now"?

Poetry presents special problems. Not the least of these is that those who translate it are usually very minor poets who cannot think of enough good lines and images to write memorable poems of their own. They need the stimulation of great poetry to get into a state of mind in which a few nice lines and images do come to them, and then they gain a public for these by putting them into their translations. The great poets obviously do not need such little favors. But even as the modern philosopher does not ask what the classical philosophers whom he interprets might have thought of him, the modern translator has excellent reasons for not asking what the great poet might have thought of the presents bestowed on him at the cost of his own lines of imagery. In the classroom, in papers, and in conversations held years later, discussions of great poets are based on versions of this type. (See section 29 above.)

Perhaps I may be forgiven for quoting briefly from "A Note on Translations" at the end of my *Tragedy and Philosophy* (1968):

> In 1965 Sartre published *Les Troyennes,* an adaptation of Euripides' *Trojan Women.* Soon an 'English version' of this adaptation appeared, and the vast audience that reads Sartre in English might have turned to this attractively produced volume to see how Sartre had changed Euripides' play. But on page xvii we are brought up short: "I have taken as many liberties with M. Sartre as he has with Euripides." This surely approximates a *reductio ad absurdum.* . . . This case is extreme, for in the end we get neither Sartre nor Euripides but Ronald Duncan.

In the case of a play there may be the hope—or if the translation is commissioned by the BBC even the promise—that the new version will be performed. But unless it is filmed or videotaped, it seems clear that once the text is printed, far more people will read the new version than will ever see it on the stage, and most of the readers will be students who will then go on to discuss the original author on the basis of the modern version. And this is rather like discussing ancient art without ever as much as looking at it, making do instead with rather free copies in a style that is more-modern.

In the case of sculpture and painting, architecture and music, the very suggestion sounds grotesque. But in the case of drama and poetry, as well as some other forms of literature, this is widely held to be no more than common sense. Hardly anyone seems to have noticed how much all of this is like studying Gothic architecture on the basis of late-nineteenth-century versions of the Gothic on American campuses.

It may be objected that in music we do rely on contemporary interpretations. But music is different in many ways. It is usually played for pleasure, and anyone *teaching* Bach or Mozart should certainly explain to students how eighteenth-century performances differed from modern ones. Moreover, thousands of people who love music compare different interpretations entirely on their own, by listening to different recordings. In the case of literature, however, even teachers rarely compare different translations, and students are hardly ever asked to make such comparison. They should be. It would be a very instructive assignment to ask students to "translate" a passage from Shakespeare in the manner of the Revised Standard Version, the New English Bible, and some of the more renowned translations of various classics. This would make students aware of the meaning of style, and they would begin to understand what happens in translations.

In addition, students of music should hear Bach and Mozart played on eighteenth-century instruments, and they should see Greek tragedies performed with masks, and Shakespearean tragedies with all the roles played by men. With records, tapes, and videotapes, this could easily be arranged, and if financial subsidies were needed, foundations and governments should realize how much such projects would benefit the humanities.

To subsidize modern adaptations of old plays or novels on television does as much for the humanities as would subsidies for "contemporary" versions of Greek or Gothic buildings. Any money spent to help the humanities in this way does positive harm. The point is not that such buildings cannot be pleasing or that such productions cannot be entertaining. Of course, they can be; but in the process of pleasing and entertaining they promote a lack of discrimination and understanding. The result is that people think that they know what they do not know—say, Euripides—and that what they think they know is wildly wrong.

People are willing to follow television cameras into the most exotic places to see in their natural habitat animals that one had never hoped to see outside a zoo; and the more we are shown things the like of which we had never seen before, the better we like it. But when the BBC brings Ibsen's plays to television audiences, it obliterates whatever might appear a little strange and turns them into soap operas about the British middle class. And that is widely hailed as a major triumph of educational television. Is it any wonder when students with a taste for adventure and excitement prefer the sciences to the humanities?

When one of his students gave up mathematics to become a novelist, David Hilbert (1862–1943), one of the greatest mathematicians of recent times, said that it was just as well; the young man did not have enough imagination to do anything interesting in mathematics. The remark was quoted often because it struck so many people as paradoxical. Surely, it has lost its air of paradox.

In our colleges and universities, there are no departments that share a monopoly on imagination, and it is arguable that important work in any field requires imagination. It is also arguable that it is a raison d'être of the humanities to deal with the works fashioned by the human imagination and to stimulate and enlarge the imagination of students. Works that come from other cultures and, in the case of literature, from other languages have an especially important role in this connection. Hence it will not do to discuss the art of reading without going on to speak of translations. We need translations, but the versions we get are often counter-productive.

When we deal with great poetry or with writers who had a truly distinctive style, the translator's problems may appear to be insoluble. That they are difficult is undeniable, but once we realize that a problem of ethics is involved and to whom the translator is responsible, some solutions can be found.

36

First of all, translators owe their authors and their readers some account of the nature of the new version and of the qualities of the original that have got lost to some extent, of the writer's style and some of the special problems posed by it. This accounting is the translator's province and is badly needed by the student, in a postscript if not in the preface. There is certainly no harm in also telling the reader something about the writer's life and works and thought, although information of that kind is almost always easily available elsewhere. It is helpful to have it summarized in the same volume with the new version, but the accounting is really indispensable, for that cannot be found anywhere else.

Publishers may tell a translator that he is not the one to make comparisons between his own version and earlier attempts, assuming that his version is not the first. Yet in such cases the reader has a right to know why it was considered important to redo the work instead of tackling something not translated yet. One wants to know what, if anything, was felt to be inadequate in earlier attempts and what the translator tried to accomplish.

Second, there are usually some words that are especially important. In a philosophical work there are key terms on which the argument depends; in literary works, both prose

and poetry, one often finds *Leitworte* (a term coined by
Martin Buber and Franz Rosenzweig in connection with
their German version of the Hebrew Bible), meaning guid-
ing words that have the function of a leitmotif. If the translator fails to find an equivalent word that can be used consistently, a great deal may be lost—indeed, sometimes so
much that the whole version becomes useless.

The German *Geist* has no perfect equivalent in English,
but if in a philosophical work we should render it now as
spirit and now as mind, and sometimes as ghost, wit, and
intellect, we would make it impossible for students as well
as others who rely on our version to discuss the author's
conception of *Geist* or his attitude toward reason without
misconstruing many passages.

An example from Sophocles' *Antigone* may show how
the same principle applies to poetry. In the most widely
used and respected English version of *The Complete Greek
Tragedies*, the most famous line in this play is rendered:

> Many the wonders but nothing walks stranger than man.

This is actually better than a mechanical application of my
principle which might result in the line Erich Fromm has
used as a motto:

> Wonders are many, and none is more wonderful than
> man.

The fact that the Greek has *deina* and *deinoteron* does not
make this rendering right. Actually,

> Much is strange but nothing stranger than man

would come far closer to Sophocles' meaning. How can we
know? How can we help reading our own view of man into
Sophocles? For a start, we might note that the same Greek
word occurs a third time only nine lines earlier, where *The*

Complete Greek Tragedies translates it quite reasonably as
"terrible":

> How terrible to guess, and guess at lies!

Now it is not easy at all to find an English word that will
serve well in all three places. Nor is that necessarily sufficient. One has to check whether the word also occurs elsewhere in the play, in other Sophoclean tragedies, and in
earlier works—say, by Aeschylus—which may be echoed
here. This involves a great deal of work to render a single
word, though classical philologists have long compiled reference works that make it feasible to do all this. But if the
translator cannot find a word that is totally satisfactory, if
neither "dire" nor "awesome" seems ideal, it does not
follow at all that the labor was wasted. This brings us to the
third point.

There are bound to be passages that cannot be translated
without something of importance being lost. There are two
good ways of coping with them. Key terms and *Leitworte*
can and should be discussed in the translator's introduction.
Here the reader can be alerted to what is lost and to what has
been attempted. But there are many points that are not likely
to stay in one's mind until one comes to the relevant passage. One needs the information on the same page with the
text. It is extraordinary that even in a culture in which
footnotes are prized beyond all reason and abound in places
where they serve only to advertise the author's pedantry,
footnotes are hardly ever employed by translators in cases of
this kind. Yet here the added information is needed badly on
the same page and cannot be given in the text. A play on
words, a joke that can't be rendered in another language,
and important ambiguities sometimes cry out for footnotes.

In some cases much is to be said for footnote commentaries. Many translators, of course, do not know their author

well enough, but the minimal footnotes advocated here
ought to be standard fare. They would be feasible even in
the case of poetry, though there it is preferable to print the
original on facing pages. Where that is not feasible, as in
most versions of Greek poetry, footnotes could greatly enhance the value of translations of Homer and Greek tragedy.
In the case of Aristophanes as well as Lao-tze this has
actually been tried and proved most helpful.

Why have these things not become standard practice long
ago? The reasons are clear and disreputable. As much as
possible, many publishers have tried to present translations
as if they were not translations. Translators were underpaid
outrageously, and in reviews they were, perhaps more often
than not, deemed unworthy of mention—even at the top
where the names of the author and the publisher were listed
along with the title and the price. Translators were considered anonymous hacks. In the case of poetry, including the
Greek classics, the situation was not that bad, but one still
tried to give the impression that what the buyer was getting
was a timeless classic and not one of countless competing
versions by a very minor modern poet who in places could
not help—or did not mind—diverging from the major poet
he translated. Honesty was subordinated to other considerations, and the very notion that there might be an ethics of
translating did not occur to many people.

Most scholastics are not cut out to translate authors remarkable for their brilliant style, not to speak of poets. But
scholastics could contribute a great deal more than most of
them ever do if only they would furnish careful translations,
with notes and indices, of works that lack stylistic distinction. To that end, of course, one must first of all be
thoroughly at home in at least two languages. Scholars who
know Latin and Greek thoroughly have not only furnished
many helpful translations into modern languages but have
also compiled invaluable dictionaries and other reference

works. In the humanities there is ample room for hard-working scholastics, and the visionaries need their help.

37

Editing, like translating, has been discussed in passing in the context of the art of reading. But it has become such an industry, and governments and foundations in some countries are sinking so much money into it, on the assumption that this is what the humanities need, that we should consider the problems in some detail.

It may be useful to distinguish two kinds of editions that are open to criticism. The first comprises collections of articles by various hands that are brought together for classroom use. Some volumes of this kind are enormously useful. Others have plainly been conceived by hapless academics who can see no other way to publish a book over their name. Projects of this kind are often really pathetic, and most publishers probably turn down quite a few of them for every ill-conceived and pointless one they publish. But even collections that make sense can still be harmful.

Most collections of this kind that deal with a central theme include quite a few articles of very dubious value, and often more than half of the material is of this kind. The editors comb the journals for enough articles to constitute a volume of a certain size; they may feel that by representing more authors they may win more class adoptions; and they sometimes hope to curry favor with the authors they include. But what matters is not the motivation; it is the result. What is read more and more even in courses in the humanities is ephemeral material culled from journals, timely things instead of timeless classics.

What is wrong with feeding students too much timely stuff is not so much that it gives little nourishment and, though reprinted in a book, still becomes stale as fast as do old journals. It is rather that the time spent on material of this sort is taken away from books that ought to have been read. Even if junk foods, like sugared cereal products, potato chips, and soda pops, should not be harmful in themselves, those who are taught to fill up on them at the expense of more nutritious foods are ill brought up.

The second kind of edition would seem to go to the opposite extreme. I mean the so-called critical editions of the works of major figures. This is the type that has become a heavily subsidized industry. Here we are not dealing with a man here and a woman there who are fighting for academic survival by at least editing a paperback, or with professors who occasionally edit a collection on the side, but with a series of establishments that provide work for many.

While reviewers and translators often have a journalistic ethos, this kind of editing is almost invariably done by scholastics. Since the works they edit were usually written by visionaries, it is a besetting fault of most critical editions that they show extraordinarily little feeling for the author. The ancients spoke of a mountain that was in labor and brought forth a mouse. What we are witnessing is rather how colonies of ants bury giants under unsightly hills that are of use mainly to the ants who live there.

Yeats's poem "The Scholars," from which I have quoted in section 8, comes to mind, but perhaps Einstein's image of the creepers is even more to the point, for they obscure the trees on which they live and climb. I am certainly not against all critical editions. The crux is whether the editors help the author speak to us, or whether they get in his way. And my charge is that all too often critical editions have an antihumanistic thrust. At the very least, this is a problem of which editors as well as those supporting projects of this kind should be aware.

In the United States the person who attacked the government's support for critical editions most visibly and fiercely was Edmund Wilson, first in two articles in *The New York Review,* in September and October 1968, and then in *The Fruits of the MLA,* a New York Review Book, 1968. (The MLA is the Modern Language Association.) I have already given my reasons for thinking that he did not have enough respect for careful scholarship, and I have never read William Dean Howells's first book, *Their Wedding Journey,* much less studied the critical edition of this work, which Wilson criticized at length. But it would seem that the National Endowment of the Humanities could have spent its funds in better ways than by subsidizing critical editions of the work of Howells. It seems safe to assume that those who made this decision had not given much thought to the question whether Howells's voice needed to be heard, and whether an edition of this sort would help it.

Tom Sawyer is certainly a classic, but assuming that the facts are as Wilson states, I do not see how one could possibly deny that much of the work done by the editors was trivial and unnecessary. According to Wilson, more than a dozen people were required to read *Tom Sawyer* backwards, lest they be distracted by the meaning or the style of the book, and they had to determine where "Aunt Polly" was spelled with a capital "A" and where with a lower case "a," and where "ssst" was spelled with three "s's" and where with four.

Is it too much to say that the humanities are adrift, and that those charged with spending large amounts of money for them have not given enough thought to goals? And that sometimes, if not usually, they listen too much to scholastics?

If the conservation and cultivation of the greatest works of the human spirit is one of the foremost goals of the humanities, it stands to reason that it is important to have good editions and translations of such works. To that end, value judgments are needed to decide what seems greater than what or, to use current idiom, to determine the priorities. If our concern is really with the humanities, it is by no means obvious that critical editions of the novels of relatively minor Americans are needed more than good translations into English of great classics that are not available in adequate translations.

What is needed, of course, will often sell and thus pay for itself. Hence the temptation is to subsidize what is not needed. And those who flock to subsidized projects of this kind are often the least likely to have any feeling for the author.

What we need is some discussion of priorities and standards for translations and editions. When a subsidy is seriously considered, one might have a competition in which those who would like to make a bid for the job would be asked to submit a sample of perhaps ten pages, indicating what they would do and why.

What is still needed, however, is some discussion of the four kinds of material with which critical editions have to cope. Each raises different problems. I shall deal briefly first with genuine works, then with *Nachlass* material (meaning things the author did not publish, such as drafts and fragments), then with letters, and finally with lectures.

38

In the case of works that a writer published in one edition only, there is generally no need whatsoever for a critical edition. A good editor can furnish a helpful introduction and add footnotes to explain some references and allusions and perhaps also call attention to some ambiguities. But all that is more in the nature of a miniature commentary and not what is usually meant by a critical edition. On the other hand, critical editions of a writer's collected works are often inflated beyond reason by the inclusion of works that are simply reprinted at horrendous prices.

Matters become complicated when a work has passed through several revised editions while the author was still living. The more editions and the more extensive the revisions, the more difficult are the editors' problems. In the case of Kant's *Critique of Pure Reason,* however, German editors long ago found very adequate ways of presenting the text of the first edition of 1781 and the variants of the second edition of 1787 in the same volume in very inexpensive popular editions. The page numbers of both versions were given on the margins, one as A, the other as B, and with no fuss, pretentiousness, or stunning apparatus the problem was solved so well that scholars and students ever since have had no difficulties quoting or checking either A or B.

In the case of works of at least remotely comparable importance, it seems highly desirable to follow this example. Shakespeare is a case in point, and some editions have long managed to produce the variants in footnotes. The poems of Yeats are also available in one volume, complete with variants. Always, the accent ought to be on readability and handiness. In rare cases the best solution may be to reprint both the first and the last edition in their entirety, with footnotes that call attention to the differences, explaining also where various intermediate editions differ from both versions.

What is crucial is that one should ask before embarking on the enterprise what its purpose is to be. When there is reason to feel that the work and the differences between various editions are so important that students should not study the text without taking into account all of these variants, the central purpose of the edition is defeated when the volume that is produced becomes all but unreadable, and outrageously expensive to boot.

When the idea is rather that specialists in the field should be apprized of the differences between various editions, and this simply can't be done in any way that would produce a readable volume, it should be seriously considered whether the information could not be given better and in more usable form in an article. But cases of this sort are few and far between.

It is the *Nachlass,* the material a writer himself left behind unpublished when he died, that is the staple of critical editions. The big question is always *what* to publish. The uncritical answer of most editors of critical editions is: *everything.* Why? To what purpose? The problem becomes acute only when the amount of material is vast, but cases are not lacking where it is anticipated that the completion of such critical editions is bound to require decades. Meanwhile, the editors and sponsors often feel that the whole enterprise would be undercut if scholars could consult and publish some of this material while the work is still in progress. In such cases, the apparent horror of anything that could be construed as censorship results in censorship.

What would serve the cause of scholarship far better would be a critical sifting of the vast materials and early publication of any hitherto unknown fragments or passages that may throw new light on the author. This is what was done with *Hegels theologische Jugendschriften* (1907) and Marx's early manuscripts (1932), to mention two outstanding examples. But this is usually precisely what is not done, leaving one to wonder if there really is anything at all that does require interesting reinterpretations. If there isn't, the whole enterprise is dubious.

In any case it seems clear what critical editors should do. They should first of all give the public an account of what there is that has not been published before, including a detailed description and identification of every item. In this way all interested scholars would be informed at the outset what was available, and they could either come to the archives and look at items of special concern to them or request photocopies. Surely that would be preferable to the present system in which enormously expensive volumes are published at great intervals. The system now followed is clearly not designed to disseminate interesting information as rapidly, as cheaply, and as efficiently as possible.

What really should be published are provisional articles, calling attention to discoveries, and selected texts that seem especially important. Where discoveries involve unpublished texts, these texts should be published. In every case the editors should explain why they publish what, and what, if anything, they omit and why. As long as any scholar could request copies of omitted portions, there would be no danger of underhanded censorship.

39

In the case of *letters,* too, it rarely makes much sense to insist on the publication of all the letters that an author ever wrote and received, especially when the numbers involved are so large that they would fill many volumes. What is called for is, once again, a critical selection, which could be preceded by an account of how many letters to and from each correspondent are available, including the dates and length of each. Again copies could be made available to interested scholars. In some cases it could be stated that the family of the author or of one of the correspondents did not permit copies to be made available until such and such a time. For the same reason—or on account of highly embarrassing references to third parties—some passages in publishable letters might be omitted. Some academic voyeurs might be upset by that, but the present system would serve them no better. On the contrary.

There is another reason for selection. Most people find themselves in situations where they have to write a lot of dull business letters, and at other times they have to inform different correspondents of the same events. A writer is ill served by being made to look tedious and repetitious on that account.

In Germany volumes of letters sometimes sell well; in the United States they rarely do. But our concern here is not with what people may find entertaining in their leisure time and with what may or may not make a publisher some money. From the point of view of scholarship and education letters are important, if at all, for the light they throw on a writer's work, thought, and mentality, and in rarer cases also on his time. From this point of view, and indeed in almost every way, the demand for completeness rarely makes sense, and vast, enormously expensive, multivolume editions that take years to bring out are usually counterproductive.

An archive may aim to make "everything" available; books require editorial judgment. Here are some of the options an editor confronts. One can try to publish all of a writer's letters in chronological order. In most cases this will result in an immensely repetitious and unreadable series of volumes, and in the absence of copious notes providing information about the letters that the writer was answering, many texts will be misleading if not incomprehensible. Interspersing all of the correspondents' letters to the writer in an edition of this sort is not feasible. Fitting them in under their own datelines would produce chaos and render the whole enterprise virtually unreadable. Only a selection of the letters that a writer wrote and received can be presented in a single chronological sequence that makes sense.

The two Italian editors of the critical edition of Nietzsche's works and letters that is being published in Berlin have found an ingenious solution. They have decided to publish *all* of Nietzsche's cards and letters in chronological order in six and a half volumes, and *all* extant cards and letters to him also in six and a half volumes, in chronological sequence. The first volume, which begins with Nietzsche at the age of five and ends before his twentieth birthday, contains the material he wrote, including many such items as "Nietzsche requests permission to purchase ink," on pages 1–297, and the material written to him on pages 299–436. After that, the letters from Nietzsche and to him are presented in separate volumes. A selection of letters about Nietzsche will comprise four volumes, and the editorial apparatus three more, making for a total of twenty volumes.

All this makes sense only when an author did not write too many routine letters, and when he did not receive hundreds of trivial and uninteresting letters. What percentage of the letters Nietzsche got were of some interest remains to be seen. Although the edition was first announced many years ago, the first three volumes appeared only in 1975.

The reasons given by the editors to explain their desire for completeness, even when it comes to the mail Nietzsche received, are mainly three:

a) all "voices" that ever "reached" Nietzsche shall be included;
b) a selection would inevitably conjure up the danger of subjective interpretation and thus
c) seriously call into question the desired definitiveness of a critical total edition of the correspondence.

Undeniably, a banal letter *may* turn out to throw some light on a passage in another letter or a book, and a lot of trivial letters may add up to a striking picture of the milieu of a writer. It would be premature to judge this particular endeavor. But it seems clear that it would make very little sense to publish all the letters Freud received, not to speak of William Dean Howells or Dwight Eisenhower. Nietzsche evidently received relatively little mail, and he lived such a lonely life that a disproportionate number of the voices that reached him came by mail. Even so, there were others, too. Most of what he read was after all not mail.

Let us assume that Nietzsche's case is exceptionally favorable for a "critical total edition," also because few writers since 1800 were so interesting and influential. Even then some serious problems remain. First and most important, all the books he wrote have been issued in two volumes on thin paper. If it were not for these books, his letters would not be of any interest to anybody, and the very thought of publishing the letters sent to him would be absurd. It would seem that those interested in Nietzsche should above all read and study the books he wrote. But now they are invited to divide their time and energy between the books, the *Nachlass,* and the letters, not to speak of secondary literature. Hardly anyone has time enough for Nietzsche to digest all that, and what naturally happens for the most part is that the time spent on the nonbooks comes out of the time that might well have been spent on Nietzsche's books. In this way, what is most significant always tends to be drowned in a sea of what is relatively insignificant. To vary the metaphor slightly: Nietzsche's voice is drowned out by the voices that addressed him and that talked about him.

Moreover, to make proper use of such a critical edition one must have four large volumes open at the same time: one each with letters from Nietzsche, to him, and about him, and a fourth in which the editors supply, along with data about the manuscripts, the vital information that one often needs to understand the texts. For obvious reasons, the volumes with the editorial apparatus always appear later, usually a great many years later, and meanwhile the reader is hampered at every turn, not even knowing who some of the writers are.

When the job is done as carefully as the Italian editors have done it, without large subsidies and a big staff, motivated by a desire for philological cleanliness, we have reason to be grateful. And putting the editorial notes into separate volumes may make the text volumes less subjective and more definitive. Still, I feel that the reader would be served far better if vital notes were offered on the pages where one needs them.

This has been done admirably in *The Freud/Jung Letters: The Correspondence between Sigmund Freud and C. G. Jung,* edited—superbly—by William McGuire, in a single volume (1974). The inclusion of all extant letters by both men makes one realize how much would be lost if we had only the letters written by one of them; and having the editor's copious notes where they are needed makes all the difference.

Jung writes Freud on December 7, 1912, that he has "designs on reviewing [Alfred] Adler's book. I have succeeded in descending into its depths, where I found some delightful things that deserve to be hung aloft. The man really is slightly dotty." That seems only moderately interesting until one reads in a note that in the foreword to one of his own books Jung had written in the fall of 1912 that Adler's book had come to his attention "only after the preparation of these lectures," and "I recognize that he and I have reached similar conclusion on various points." Jung "did not, so far as is known, publish a review," but "he gave not unfavourable treatment to the book and to Adler's theories generally in . . . Sept. 1913. . . ."

Notes obviously require discrimination, lest what is important be drowned out by trivia. This calls both for a thorough knowledge of the lives and writings of the letter writers—a tall order in the case of Freud and Jung—and enough detachment to allow the editor to be selective in his notes without being tendentious. In both respects, William McGuire has set standards that few editors will ever equal. But if the job can be done that well in a singularly hard case, there is little excuse for not trying in the many cases that are easier.

40

Apart from *The Freud/Jung Letters,* Freud's and Jung's letters have been treated differently. A selection of Jung's letters has been published in two volumes (three in the original German which, however, do not contain any more letters). One volume of almost six hundred pages extends from 1906 to 1950, another, which is a little bulkier, covers the last ten years of Jung's life (1951–61). He was born in 1875, but there are no letters before 1906, and few before 1930.

This selection represents an immense labor of love; and this is also true of the notes, which appear on the pages where they are needed. Even if one is very much interested in Jung, one is not likely to feel that either he or the reader would have been served better by a much larger selection of letters he wrote after 1930, much less by the publication of all letters he received. Of course, there are a few particular letters that should have been included, but we may hope that, once they are called to the editor's attention, they will be added in the next edition.

Just as the first copies of volume two were sent out by the publisher, J. A. Stargardt in Marburg, the most important German firm dealing in autographs, mailed out a catalogue (#608) that included twenty-seven letters and cards that Jung had written to a German psychotherapist, Wolfgang Kranefeldt. In its usual scholarly way, the firm describes the lot, piece by piece (p. 14f.), and it would seem that at the very least one letter will have to be included in future editions. On February 9, 1934, Jung wrote Kranefeldt in Germany that although nothing could be done against stupidity the Aryans could after all call the attention of the German government to the fact that Freud's and Adler's points of view, which were still being propagated publicly, were specifically Jewish and demonstrably *zersetzend*. If Jung's family granted permission to publish this letter, an editorial footnote might point out that *zersetzend* was a word the Nazis constantly associated with the Jews. There is no precise English equivalent, but "disintegrative" comes close. Jung went on to say that while nothing further could be done if the spread of these Jewish gospels pleased the German government, it was possible after all that the government might not be pleased.

Freud's executors published first his letters to Fliess, covering the years from 1887 to 1902, and in the title of that volume called attention to the fact that the aim was to illuminate *The Origins of Psychoanalysis*. Regard for Freud was subordinated to regard for what might be of scientific interest. The letters Fliess had written were no longer extant, and Freud himself had not wanted his own letters to be published.

This volume was followed by a beautiful selection of Freud's letters, from 1873 to his death in 1939, in which Freud stood revealed as one of the finest letter writers of all time—at least in the original German. And then there appeared several collections in the style of *The Freud/Jung Letters*, each containing his correspondence with someone of special interest: Oskar Pfister, Karl Abraham, Arnold Zweig, Lou Andreas-Salomé. In every one of these volumes one finds the whole man, without much ado, and each paid for itself.

In this way Nietzsche's correspondence with Franz Overbeck, his loyal friend who was a professor of church history at Basel University, but an unbeliever, was published in 1916. A few omissions were indicated at the time but not explained. Since then a man who disliked Nietzsche but wrote six books on him, winning an audience for each by including previously unpublished documents, included the omitted passages in his last book, in 1963. It would make good sense to reissue—and even to translate—this correspondence, complete, also in paperback. It would throw more light on Nietzsche than any of the several editions of selected letters that have been published in English.

In a sense a *kritische Gesamtausgabe* is a contradiction in terms, although the term is much in use in Germany. "Total" editions are in an important sense uncritical; for being critical involves discrimination. This problem is nicely pointed up by the phrase already quoted once: "A selection would inevitably conjure up the danger of subjective interpretation." Surely, this "danger" is unavoidable when one chooses to be critical; and for good measure, Nietzsche would have thought it was unavoidable in any case. For the reasons indicated earlier, it may be true nevertheless that Nietzsche's correspondence is so unusual that the "critical total edition" of it will become a treasure trove. If so, it still should be regarded as a rare exception and not as a model to be followed.

41

Lectures pose no special problems when the writer himself has put them down on paper. When he did not and someone else took notes, one would not usually think of publishing those, and one would scarcely presume to flesh them out and present the result as one of the writer's major works. But in the case of Hegel something much worse has been done.

He published only four works, of which the last two were terse syllabi consisting of consecutively numbered sections, averaging well under one very uncrowded page in length.

On the title pages of the last two books, his *Encyclopedia* and *Philosophy of Right,* he stated clearly that they were intended for his students, to be used in connection with his lectures. Both volumes could be read through quickly to gain something of an overview, but were hard to understand in detail. During the last ten years of his life he became a very influential professor and did not publish any more books. But four years before his death he brought out a very radically revised second edition of the *Encyclopedia* (his system), which had originally appeared ten years earlier; and the year before he died he published a third edition, again radically revised.

Hegel's lectures were hard to follow. He composed his long and often tortuous sentences as he went along, and his voice was neither strong nor clear. His major courses, including the vastly influential lectures on the philosophy of history, he gave repeatedly, but they were never the same twice. He usually recast the whole course, never being satisfied even with his overall organization, not to speak of individual sentences.

After his death, his students decided to publish his collected works, including his lectures. Some of the most trenchant comments he had made in lecturing on his syllabi they printed as "additions" to the numbered sections of the final, third edition of his system, which had appeared shortly before his death. But for ten years the lectures had actually been based on the first edition, and then for three years on the second. The editors had to find appropriate places for the sentences they chose to print, and they drew on lecture notes by various hands, taken down in different years. The form of the sentences and the connections between them were admittedly sometimes due to the editors.

With these additions the *Encyclopedia,* a book of roughly three hundred very uncrowded pages in the first edition, and twice that in the third, became an imposing work compris-

ing three tomes that hardly anyone, except some very dedi-
cated Hegel scholars, ever read from beginning to end.
Even when Hegelianism flourished in England and in the
United States in the last century, the second tome never was
translated. Finally, about one hundred forty years after
Hegel's death, two English versions of the second volume
appeared simultaneously, and one of them comprised three
tomes because the translator had added so many erudite
comments to the material that in the first edition had come
to less then eighty pages and in the third to twice that.

We still do not have a one-volume translation of Hegel's
one-volume system. But if the whole work were translated
the way its second part was, Hegel's single volume would
become eleven or twelve tomes in English. Thus we are
moving from the time when books were read to an age in
which editions are consulted, and writers are buried under
colossal monuments that it will require generations to complete.

Even the first edition of Hegel's collected works contained four "works" that consisted entirely of his students'
lecture notes. Taken together, they were twice as long as the
four works Hegel had published. But the early editors tried
hard to make the master readable and succeeded so well that
many people have turned to this material because it is so
much more easily accessible than Hegel's books.

The first attempts to produce "critical" editions of Hegel
were still produced in inexpensive volumes and designed for
use by students as well as specialists. Georg Lasson
supplied superb introductions and immensely helpful footnotes; and a generation later, after World War II, Johannes
Hoffmeister still worked in this tradition, revising and adding to Lasson's splendid editions.

That was before the notion of the *kritische Gesamtausgabe* was fully developed. In those bygone days one still

asked oneself about the purpose of such publications and was clear about one's primary responsibility to Hegel and to students and professors. Now governments and foundations have been persuaded, by no means only in Germany, that they should subsidize a minor industry to erect public monuments.

Again, it is arguable that Hegel represents a very special case. Partly owing to the worldwide interest in Marx, interest in Hegel has grown to the point where any volume that contains new Hegel material is bound to be used, or at least consulted, by scholars in many countries, even if hardly anyone should read it from cover to cover. After all, well over a thousand books and articles on him were published in the period from 1970 to 1975. Almost all of this vast literature is, of course, scholastic and makes it harder and harder to approach the "audacious, profound and devastating, at times wildly turbulent thinker," to cite Isaiah Berlin's characterization of Hegel.

42

The point at issue has been put well by Gregory Vlastos, finding fault in a review with the attempt of another leading classicist, W. K. C. Guthrie, who had been bold enough to devote to Plato two volumes of *A History of Greek Philosophy*. This undertaking, said Vlastos in the London *Times Literary Supplement* (December 12, 1975), "is so stupendous that anyone but the most intrepid scholar would have fled from it in terror." Why?

> While only scraps of the earlier Greek philosophizing have survived, all of Plato's oeuvre has—indeed quite a lot more: some twenty-eight pseudepigrapha, several of them still thought genuine by some scholars, have swelled the ancient canon of his works. To acquire a thorough knowl-

edge of this corpus could well be all by itself the task of a lifetime. But that would be only the first item on the historian's agenda.

Indeed, if that were all, one might well interpose that Plato's works are after all available in English in a single handy volume, on thin paper, that includes even some of the material that Vlastos does not consider genuine; and if it would require a lifetime to master that, then no scholar should dare to deal even in a multivolume work with writers whose *oeuvre* is far larger, as is that of Luther, Kant, and Goethe, or of Freud and Jung, to mention but a few names.

When it comes to those who influenced Plato—the second item on the agenda—the situation is even more favorable in his case because so little has survived. But the crux of this critique of Guthrie's first volume on Plato is what Vlastos calls "the mountainous heap of modern comment and comment on comment." More than two thousand titles of secondary works, including articles, of course, have been listed for

> the 1950–57 stretch. . . . But bulk alone will hardly show the difficulty of assimilating this vast accumulated product of learned industry. More intimidating than its bulk is the diversity of skills and procedures. . . . Is it humanly possible for all this to be mastered by a single brain capable of decoding all its jargons . . . ? I shall believe it only when I see it. It has not been done in this volume.

These remarks would not be half so poignant if the writer were not widely known as a leading humanist. As it is, anyone who henceforth tries to deal with the achievements of a major figure in two volumes, instead of confining himself more cautiously to some details, will have to be doubly intrepid. And it should be clear how the editors of vast critical editions as well as those who use their highly specialized skills and procedures to write about details contribute their share to "the mountainous heap" that stands in the way of any overall assessment.

This is unfortunate not only when we deal with truly great thinkers. While the literature on existentialism keeps growing at an alarming rate, those who contribute to it give no signs of having noticed that Martin Heidegger was like a character thought up by Kierkegaard. On the occasion of Heidegger's eighty-fifth birthday in 1974, it was announced that his "works" would be published in seventy volumes. The completion of this enterprise is expected to take many, many decades. In the foreseeable future, then, any critic of Heidegger's immense pretentions is likely to be met with the claim that it is much too early to assess the man, and "anyone but the most intrepid scholar" will flee "in terror," while some scholastics spend their lives editing Heidegger. And if the task should ever be completed, and the scholarly community is faced with seventy volumes of "works" plus heaps and heaps of monographs and monographs on monographs, what critic, feeling that Heidegger was importantly wrong or misguided, would want to spend his life digesting all that before venturing to prove his point?

Moreover, what the editors of critical editions give us is often grossly misleading, even when their intentions are the best. Drafts and notes are usually full of corrections. Much is crossed out, sometimes still legible and sometimes not; much is inserted between lines or on the margins, top, or bottom of the page; and frequently words and abbreviations cannot be deciphered with assurance. When all this is indicated faithfully, the text becomes unreadable; when some of it is indicated but not all, the text becomes misleading. Most editions of material of this sort are utterly inadequate in one way or another and give the reader no idea of the fluid character of the manuscript. Typically, there is a great show of enormous carefulness that makes the page so hard to read that one can scarcely concentrate on what is said; and yet, when one compares it with the manuscript or a facsimile, the printed text is seen to have omitted some of the most interesting information.

Interlarding complete facsimiles in critical editions would make them still more expensive. Critics of the critical editions sponsored by the Modern Language Association in the United States have called drafts a writer's "garbage." In some cases—not in most—it may be worthwhile to study a draft or a manuscript full of corrections; but the best solution is surely to make photocopies of some sort available to scholars who request them. Our technology has not made obsolete books, which have many advantages, but we should seriously inquire whether it has not made obsolete "critical total editions."

43

The central question about any edition concerns its purpose. What is wanted? What revelations are hoped for or expected? Is our concern indiscriminately antiquarian? Or do some people find a special thrill in reading what a writer did not publish and never intended for the eyes of others? Why should foundations and governments cater to such Peeping Toms?

Ultimately, the elephantiasis of these vast editions and the microscopism that characterizes so much of the other work done in the humanities have similar results and the same cause. Both lead to triviality and loss of meaning. Both issue from the failure to inquire about the purpose of one's work.

This failure is excused implausibly by saying that it is Philistine to ask about the purpose of one's work, and that the search for truth is an end in itself. If that were true, we might as well fund institutes for the study of nineteenth-century postage stamps and endow chairs for the chemical analysis of their dyes. Not only those who fund projects but also individual scholars and students have to choose among projects; and those who simply keep amassing data, facts, or information without having in mind questions to which they are seeking a solution are almost bound to produce trivial work. Those who work without a purpose contribute to the growing sense that work is meaningless.

What one edits or translates—or reviews, for that matter—is the work of a writer, and one should begin by asking: Why this writer rather than that one? And why this work rather than that? What is the point of it? What makes it worth publishing? *Cui bono?* Whom is it likely to profit?

The hack's answer is simple: Myself! I am getting paid for it. And a publisher may say, and often does say: I hope it will make money. But a scholar cannot simply plead: I am following the truth wherever it may lead. That is not why one chooses one project rather than another. And a psychologist might even say, though there is a dearth of the kind of psychologists who would say: So far from following the truth and exploring explosive issues, the translator or editor, not to speak of reviewers, may well be a person who is playing it safe by burying himself in the work of someone else, more of a drudge than an adventurer.

The obvious reason for translating or editing is to make available to others something one considers especially beautiful or important—a work that says something vital that should not be ignored. It may be new information or a new way of seeing things, a striking criticism of accepted views, or perhaps a book, fragment, or sequence of letters that places a person, a movement, or a period in a new light. (A reviewer might do well to ask, too, if this is the case.) And when previous translations or editions are seriously misleading, one may choose to do a new one for the same reasons, or perhaps to facilitate a reinterpretation of the author. In every case, the editor or translator should tell the reader what the purpose of the project was, and reviewers ought to discuss the purpose and evaluate its execution.

I argued in the last chapter that a good interpreter needs to have some grasp of the mentality—the *geistige Persönlichkeit*—of the author, and it is obvious how valuable a writer's *Nachlass* and letters can be in this context. More often than not, however, as I have tried to show, translations and "total" editions obscure the writer. Translations are typically too unfaithful, while "total" editions tend to smother the writer with fanatical, misguided faithfulness. The "works" gradually become so voluminous and cumbersome that hardly anyone, except for a few drudges whom the writer would have found completely uncongenial and who have never felt even a breath of his spirit, can digest the *corpus;* and those who have time for only a few volumes divide that between some of his books and the more numerous nonbooks. Thus material that an author never thought of publishing competes for attention with the works to which he gave his life.

The tendency is the same as that of scholastic microscopism; more and more people lose sight of the wood for the trees in it. Legions are living off dead writers instead of giving them of their own blood to make them speak.

Homer already knew that the dead can speak only after drinking blood; but Odysseus got by with the blood of sheep. Today sheep will no longer do, nor will human sweat. None of the dead who are worth listening to can be wooed with sweat, and they are loath to reveal their inmost thoughts and their personalities to scholars who shrink from the dangers of subjectivity. The writers, composers, and artists of the past without whom there would not be any humanities departments were people of passion, people who loved and perhaps also hated; and anyone who would like to make them speak must be congenial to them at least in some measure. That rules out self-indulgence and the lazy subjectivity that says simply, "I think," or still worse, "I should like to think." One must sacrifice some of one's dearest illusions and hopes and offer the dead one's very own blood.

CHAPTER FOUR: THE PLACE OF RELIGION IN HIGHER EDUCATION

44

There was a time in India and in Israel, in the Arab world and in Europe, when religion was central in higher education or even its be-all and end-all. In medieval Europe the schoolmen who taught at the universities were monks, and in the early twentieth century Woodrow Wilson was the first president of Princeton University who was not a clergyman. Compulsory daily chapel services survived at many American colleges until well after Wilson's time, and compulsory attendance at Sunday services was not abolished in many of them until well after World War II. Before the cornerstone for the new university library at Princeton was laid in June 1947, an enormous pit was dug to ensure that the new building would not be as tall as the nearby chapel which, it was felt, must remain the highest building on the campus. After compulsory chapel was abolished, however, the chapel became—most of the time—an empty shell, its size as anachronistic as its Gothic architecture. Even during the days of compulsory attendance, it was easier to come by a deep emotional experience in the nearby Theatre Intime, where undergraduates occasionally mounted fine performances in a place that held about two hundred people.

Religion has gone out with Greek and Latin; a few students still study it, but the vast majority—of theists, too—is almost totally ignorant of it. It used to be assumed that one knew Latin and the Bible before entering college and that this supplied a needed basis or at least an added dimension for further studies. Now students have no Latin and less Greek; and the Old Testament no less than the New is Greek to them. Even in the days of compulsory Sunday services, students who had gone to Sunday school for ten years and signed up for an upper-class course in philosophy of religion did not know for the most part in what languages the Bible was written, could not say who Abraham was, and could not recall ever having heard of Habakkuk or of Galatians. Evidently, they had never even got as far as a table of contents of the Bible, leaving one to wonder what, if anything, they had learned in Sunday school or chapel. They had not the faintest notion when Moses might have lived, and the question who the Buddha was drew such answers as: a Chinese philosopher.

Now some special schools in some parts of the world still cater to the few for whom their own religion is even today *the* subject of higher education, but the students at these schools are vastly outnumbered by those who graduate from modern universities knowing almost nothing of religion. Superficially, this is a neat illustration of the vulgar dialectic that moves from a thesis to an antithesis, as if the eclipse of religion in higher education were due to an overemphasis a generation or two ago. But it is not the case that a generation or two ago the students were sated with too much knowledge and hence wanted no more of it. The reaction is not against too much knowledge of the Bible or of church history but against years of wretched teaching that did not manage to produce even a basic religious literacy. After a decade of exposure to Sunday school and sermons, students still knew next to nothing of their own denominations, not to speak of others, or of similar religions, or of very different ones.

It might seem as if we must go further back to see the swing of the pendulum. Certainly the Bible was better known by educated people in the nineteenth century, but they, too, had no idea when Moses might have lived or who the Buddha was. And even if they did know the creed of their own denomination, most of them knew nothing of the history either of the creed or of the denomination—and less about rival creeds and denominations, not to speak of other religions.

Ignorance has been with us for a long time. There can be no question of going back to a golden age. The question is rather whether we ought to attack this ignorance and, if so, how.

Even if we assume that knowledge is preferable to ignorance, the question is one of priorities. In something like three or four years students cannot gain knowledge of everything; education has to be exceedingly selective; and the problem is whether religion should have an important place in it or be tolerated at most like medieval Scandinavian drama.

45

The notion that religion is not a crucial subject and the view that it should be moved into the center and taught by apologists are worthy of each other, and one may well wonder which is more outrageous. The second is, if the apologists are all committed to the same religion; the first, if they represent a wide spectrum.

The reasons for this judgment have been spelled out in the first two chapters. If we want to lead our students to examine their own faith and morals and the ideologies and values of their parents, peer groups, and society, there can hardly be a more important subject than *comparative religion*.

It is in religion that faith and morals are encountered *par excellence;* and in different religions, if not in different sects and phases of the same ones, we find radically divergent faiths and moral views. Hence Socratic teachers and dialectical readers can scarcely hope to find materials that are worthier of their best efforts and more appropriate for humanistic education than religious scriptures and comparative religion generally.

The reason for at one time beginning with Latin and Greek was to give students some historical perspective and a grounding in a culture different from their own. Knowing Latin also was a help in learning Romance languages and botany, but that was not the main point. What one wished to produce was humane men of letters rather than better biologists or more men who might master Spanish and Roumanian. The idea was admirable and yet deplorably parochial. One read Homer in Greek, which was all to the good, but not the Old Testament in Hebrew; and Lao-tze and Confucius, Buddhism and Hinduism, were simply *terra incognita*. In this setting, Homer and Greek tragedy failed to produce any great culture shock. The usual approach was very genteel, unless the students got a laugh out of ribald passages in Aristophanes and a few Roman authors. After World War II, attempts to sell the classics at least in translation often stooped to the appeal to sex instead of stressing what was radically different and what was *not* to be found closer to home. Modern versions were hailed for showing that some of the ancients had been "regular guys" not so different from ourselves. The departure from stolidity and stuffiness was all to the good and also became a mark of more and more translations of the Bible, but the question of purpose was once again ignored. Why should one bother with material of this kind? As sex became ever more prominent in contemporary books, not to speak of magazines and films, the threadbareness of this attempt to sell the classics could hardly be missed.

What courses in Greek and Roman writers and in comparative literature could accomplish at least in a modest way, though they rarely did, can be achieved most easily in comparative religion. This subject might well replace the classical requirement of Greek and Latin. Indeed, we should seriously consider whether some knowledge of comparative religion should not be required of all college students along with some competence in mathematics, in the art of reading, and in writing simple, lucid prose. More ambitious schools might also demand mastery of at least one live foreign language and a term's residence in a country where that language is spoken. As it is, students are exposed to a vast amount of repetition; and fashionable authors like Camus or Wittgenstein are taught in any number of courses as long as the fashion lasts, without anybody's asking about purposes and aims.

46

It would go too far to insist that a required course in comparative religion has to continue for two semesters, or that it must be a one-term course. Ideally, if a subject is important, one might wish that its study would continue for more than two terms, but at that point specialization sets in, which is a very different thing from the desired culture shock and should be optional.

Let us consider briefly what might be done in one term and what could be done in two terms. It would be nice if one could presuppose familiarity with the Bible and concentrate on *The Sacred Books of the East*—the apt title of the fifty-volume series of English translations that Max Müller edited in the nineteenth century. But since most students do not know the Bible, and even many professors who are excited about Oriental philosophy do not, it is essential to include the Bible in comparative religion. Its importance for understanding other subjects that are widely taught makes it reasonable to devote to it fully half the course, whether it lasts one term or two. For some knowledge of the Old and New Testaments adds a dimension to the study of European and American history and literature, art, music, and philosophy.

Assuming that we had only one term of ten weeks, it would make good sense to devote three weeks to the Old Testament, two to the New, which is much shorter, and one to the Koran—which would not be time enough to read any of these works in their entirety. In the last four weeks one could read, without any omission, the Dhammapada, the Bhagavad-Gita, the Confucian Analects, and the Tao-Teh-Ching. Some of these assignments could be augmented with additional readings.

Making selections from the Bible and Koran, one should choose complete books or Suras, which again could be supplemented with a few particularly interesting passages. For three weeks of the Old Testament one might read, first, Genesis and Deuteronomy, supplemented with the first chapters of Exodus and Leviticus 19; then Micah, Isaiah, and Jeremiah; and finally Jonah, Job, and Ecclesiastes. From the New Testament one should surely read at least two Gospels—Matthew, which includes the Sermon on the Mount, and John seem a good choice—and the second week the Acts of the Apostles, Romans, and First Corinthians.

Many students, if well taught, might experience as much culture shock in reading the Bible as in exposing themselves to the scriptures of India and China. That students are able to graduate from elite institutions, having read a vast amount of drivel but never any of the books mentioned here, is certainly grotesque.

47

When two terms are available for a course in comparative religion, it makes sense to devote one of them to the Bible. Again assuming that one has ten weeks at least, the following suggestions add up to a feasible minimum. The first week might well be spent on Genesis, the second on Exodus and Deuteronomy, plus a few passages from Leviticus and Numbers. Both Books of Samuel and the First Book of Kings, if not also the Second, could easily be read the third week, while the next two weeks could be given to the Prophets. Amos, Hosea, Micah, and Isaiah—four of the great pre-exilic prophets—might be read during the fourth week, and Jeremiah, Isaiah 40–66, and Ezekiel the fifth week. Finally, a week might be given to Jonah, Job, some of the Psalms, and Ecclesiastes.

That would leave at least four weeks for the New Testament. It would be an excellent idea to begin with Mark and Matthew, Mark being the oldest of the four Gospels we have. During the second week the students would read Luke and the Acts of the Apostles, two books written by the same author. Then, Paul's Epistle to the Romans and the Gospel according to John. Paul's epistles are actually the oldest part of the New Testament, but the Gospels deal with events that are said to have happened before, Acts takes the story from the end of the Gospels to the ministry of Paul, and it has often been remarked that Paul is the hero of Acts. It is arguable that all four Gospels show Paul's influence, and it seems undeniable that John's does. Finally, in the tenth week of the course one might read First Corinthians, James, and Revelation.

In the course of the semester, students could naturally be encouraged in a variety of ways to read the whole Bible, but it would not be feasible to dwell on all of the books at equal length, and the suggestions made here are intended to show what books might be emphasized especially to give the students some idea of the range and the variety of the contents. To say that students ought to read the Bible is less helpful than more specific proposals that are of necessity more controversial.

A word still needs to be said about translations. The great virtues of the King James Bible are a commonplace, but having been "appointed to be read in churches" it deliberately flattens out the differences between the authors and their styles. The result, of course, is anything but flat. On the contrary, the tone is uniformly elevated everywhere. The effect is numbing. One feels impressed but ceases to hear what is being said, and the translators themselves did not greatly care *how* it had been said. Those who study the Bible in English have to be exposed to some samples of this version, which should be compared with other versions, including the Roman Catholic Douay Version, which is a little older, and, when the teacher has the competence to do this, with the style of the original.

Modern versions that homogenize the texts in order to make everything sound modern and colloquial are useless for our purposes, unless a teacher wants to take the time to make a few comparisons that heighten one's awareness of what is distinctive in the ancient texts. Among scholarly English versions with extensive commentaries, the Anchor Bible in more than fifty volumes, almost every one translated and edited by a different scholar, holds a special place. Still nowhere near completion over ten years after the publication of the first volume in 1964, it is obviously far from suitable for courses of this sort and was not designed for them, but it will often prove immensely helpful for the teacher.

All in all, the best version by far for courses taught in English is the Revised Standard Version. It is so readable that anyone who starts reading somewhere in the Book of Judges or in Samuel or Kings is likely to go on and on until he comes to the end of the book. The translators, however, tried to keep something of the beauty of the King James Bible while at the same time showing some awareness of the differences in style, printing poetry as poetry and prose as prose, to mention only the most obvious example. Finally, they had a scholarly conscience, and their sparse footnotes are important. A professor who knows enough can call attention to rival versions and disputed passages or even go back now and then to the original, but as a text for students this version is generally admirable. (Nevertheless, I shall abide by my practice of quoting the Bible in my own translations.)

It would serve no purpose to encumber a book written in English with similar comments on translations into other languages, but if this little volume did appear in other tongues, it would clearly be appropriate to substitute some brief discussion of translations of the Bible into those tongues for the last three paragraphs. Readers of the Bible always tend to forget how many versions of it there are, and how much depends on which one is adopted.

48

When ten weeks are available for teaching Oriental religions, one might well begin by spending one week each on the Rigveda, the Upanishads, and the Laws of Manu. The fourth week might be given to the Dhammapada and some of the Buddha's major sermons. It would be important to read some of these uncut to give the students some feeling for their tone and tempo. Next I would read the Gita, which is later and needs to be seen as a response to the challenge of the Buddha. After that the students should gain some idea of the Mahayana. The Saddharmapundarika Sutra might be a good choice for that. That would add up to six weeks on India, comparable to the six weeks on the Old Testament in the twin course.

During the next three weeks one might study first the Confucian Analects, perhaps with suitable additions; then the Tao-Teh-Ching, supplemented with some chapters from the book of Chuang-tze; and finally some Zen texts, showing what happened to Buddhism in the land of Lao-tze and Chuang-tze. The last week of the course might be spent on some Suras of the Koran.

Modern scholars are likely to feel that such a course would be bound to be superficial and that it would be far better to study one religion or, if at all possible, one text in depth. There is no doubt that it is desirable to study some text carefully at length, but that is not by any stretch of the imagination a substitute for either the one-term course or the two-term course outlined here. What the readings here described could do for students, if at all well taught, is altogether different from the benefits of a close study of one book.

An obvious case in point is the Oxford "greats" program in which Oxford undergraduates have been exposed for generations to Plato's *Republic* and Aristotle's *Nicomachean Ethics*, both in the original Greek. These books are great by any standard and worth studying in detail, but few Oxford undergraduates ever experienced any culture shock while reading them in the way in which they were read. Nor is it at all likely that a student would experience that while studying for a whole term one of the books enumerated here. The more microscopic one's study becomes, the safer is one from culture shock and any reexamination of one's life.

Obviously, the kind of curriculum suggested here would

be no guarantee that the unexamined life would not prevail after all. That would depend largely on the manner in which such courses would be taught. But if the stated reason for requiring such a course of every student were to lead the students to reflect on faith and morals and think critically about some of the most important questions, it would hardly be too much to hope that this goal could be accomplished in a large number of cases.

49

After *requiring* such a course, I would also offer as electives a few courses in which interested students could follow it up by studying some texts in depth. Again, it is grotesque that so much fashionable third-rate poetry and fiction and philosophy is scrutinized with immense care while the most profound texts of all time are scarcely looked at. It is an old story that bad currency drives out good, but there is at least some chance that good teaching of great texts would set a standard by which students might then measure lesser works. To that end it seems best to pick a text that would readily invite comparisons.

I cannot think of a better choice than Genesis. Nor do I know a book that is greater or more beautiful, profound, and influential. The brief remarks appropriate in the present context cannot begin to give any ideas of its riches. But a discussion of the place of religion in higher education should not stop short of some indication of the ways in which a Biblical book might be studied for a term. The approach I am about to develop could also be applied to other Biblical books, and some teachers might prefer to cover more ground and study several books in a single term. The crucial question is: How can one teach the Bible to young men and women who are not religious?

First of all one should try to give the student some idea of the distinctive style of Genesis and specifically of its sublime economy, which remains unsurpassed. Both earlier and later ages have often thought of majesty as necessarily ornate. It seemed to call for splendor and expansive rhetoric. The King James Bible is a case in point, though it is held in check to some extent by the original. The Hebrew Book of Genesis represents an altogether different taste and sensibility. It is not lush and gorgeous but has the austere beauty of the Sinai desert and of the scenery around Jerusalem that is littered with rocks and ancient olive trees, both riddled with holes as if everything excessive had long been eliminated. Actually, the stones do not seem to be scattered through the landscape, but the greenery is much too sparse to hide the rocky earth. Nowhere is the light more lucid and the air so clear. Nor is there any other prose that equals Genesis in its terse and simple grandeur.

The feel of the Buddha's quite deliberately repetitious sermons is utterly different, and so is, in another way, the epic joy in long descriptions that we find in Homer's *Iliad,* or again the gnomic, impish, whimsical delight in paradox that distinguishes Lao-tze. The Buddhist Dhammapada and Sophocles do not offer such extreme contrasts to the style of Genesis, and yet they, too, are different, and in a prolonged study of Genesis it would be richly worthwhile to try to bring out these differences and to relate them to the contents of the work.

Still speaking of style, one should try to bring out specifically some of the countless marvelous felicities of ever so many verses. Of course, that cannot be done on the basis of, for example, the New English Bible, which can be used nevertheless to point up some of its countless infelicities, which are doubly remarkable because in places it retains the wording of the King James Bible. It thus invites comparison with that, and it is interesting to see how the earlier version, for all its inadequacies, has a sure sense of style, rhythm, and beauty, while the modern translation does not.

Juxtapositions of a few translations of the same passages

can be very instructive. It can be a way of showing students what problems translators must solve and how greatly they differ in quality. This is an important lesson for all who constantly depend on translations and can become the beginning of critical thinking in an area in which most students never even realize that there is room for criticism. It also is a way of learning something about style and the differences between great and poor prose.

To discover the felicities of the original it is, of course, a great help if one can read it. Even those who can will find the old rabbinical commentaries and interpretations a storehouse of fascinating cases. The great majority of rabbinical exegeses will carry no conviction for an unbeliever, but even when they don't something is gained by seeing how exegetical readers have dealt with familiar texts. It is as interesting to compare different exegeses as it is to juxtapose rival translations. And occasionally the exegetes call attention to felicities that, once noted, remain unforgettable. Those without Hebrew who know German will find a wealth of examples in the Genesis translation and commentary by Benno Jacob, who was an orthodox rabbi in Berlin and drew on the accumulated work of two thousand years. Jacob's work (1934) comprises over a thousand large pages. In English there is a much briefer translation of *The Joseph Narrative in Genesis* with commentary by Rabbi Eric I. Lowenthal (1973), who drew heavily on Benno Jacob and other predecessors.

The style of Genesis is worth stressing so much not only because nothing in the world is more sublime but also because precisely the style tends to obstruct the modern reader's view of Genesis. For all its majesty, the King James Bible makes it sound remote, rhetorical, and churchly, and blinds us to its unsurpassed directness and simplicity. An excellent approach to the book is to develop first of all some sense for the writing.

50

Genesis has fifty short chapters, totaling something like sixty pages—the exact length depending on the edition. It begins with the creation of the world, related in less than forty sentences, then tells briefly of paradise and Adam's and Eve's expulsion from it, and requires not even twenty sentences to tell the timeless story of Cain and Abel. The next major part of Genesis deals with the flood and Noah, and the haunting tale of the tower of Babel takes up a mere nine verses in chapter 11. Where else have ten pages so enriched mankind's imagination?

The rest of the book deals with Abraham, his son Isaac, and with Isaac's son Jacob and his twelve sons, notably Joseph. Genesis ends with Joseph's death. There is no earlier story that rivals this tale of one family in sheer narrative power and sustained terse suggestiveness. The later account of Saul and David in the Books of Samuel, ending in the second chapter of First Kings, may equal Genesis in its gripping beauty, but it does not have the same mythical power of suggestion. The Greeks created nothing like this; nor, of course, did the Jews create anything like Homer's epics. What we have here is unique.

Jacob is the first individual in world literature who, far from being essentially a type to whose exploits one could keep adding more and more—like, say, Achilles or Odysseus—develops from youth to manhood and old age, growing in the process. After he fights with God, his name is changed to Israel, and he is thus an eponymous hero from whom the Northern Kingdom of Israel, destroyed by the Assyrians in 722 B.C., derived its name. His birth is related in chapter 25, his death in the last verse of chapter 49, and half of the book deals with him.

Teaching Genesis, one would naturally compare not only translations and exegeses but also scholarly attempts to date the work and to explain its origin. Until 1800 it was generally believed that the Torah or Pentateuch—that is, the Five Books of Moses of which Genesis is the first—had been revealed to Moses by God. In the nineteenth century any notion that the book was written by some man of genius was felt to be still too close to the old religious view, and scholars argued in all seriousness that it was wretched patchwork. They began ascribing all the verses in which God was called God (*Elohim*) to one source (E) and all those in which he was called the Lord (YHWH, now almost universally vocalized Yahweh) to another writer (J). Then one also "discovered" a priestly author (P); and as more and more German students needed to make small contributions to knowledge to obtain their doctorates, they added E_1 and E_2, J_1 and J_2, P_1 and P_2 and argued about whether any given verse or half verse ought to be assigned, for example, to E_1 or P_2. From the later nineteenth century until quite recently this sort of thing was virtually a prerequisite for academic respectability in discussions of the Five Books of Moses. It was a scissors-and-paste theory in which it was assumed by all contenders that an unexampled book had been assembled by a stupid editor who had cut up different sources, taking bits and pieces from them and gluing them together. This was supposed to explain alleged redundancies and contradictions. It was never noticed that an editor sufficiently irreverent to cut up his sources and to leave out much of each would have had to be oddly incompetent to leave us with so many alleged contradictions and redundancies; nor did one ask whether Genesis really looked like the work of an incompetent. Rarely have generations of scholastic microscopists made greater fools of themselves.

That the author of the book drew on more than one oral tradition is another matter. Sometimes he tried to find places for more than one version and did this with consummate skill. What was ridiculous was the attempt to replace the old

Mosaic theory with a mosaic theory, as if every verse and half verse could be assigned to one or another written source.

In another overreaction against the ancient Mosaic theory, some scholars claimed, and it came to be widely held, that the discovery of old Egyptian and above all Mesopotamian hymns and legends proved that Genesis was the work of copycats. Such examples merely show how grotesque intellectual fashions can be and that this does not keep them from occasionally dominating universities for generations. In this case, as often, they involved a curious double standard. Earlier the Bible had been treated as altogether different from all other books. Now it was again judged by altogether different standards. Who would have dared to call Sophocles a copycat or to explain the contradictions in the plot of his *Antigone* by claiming that the play must be the work of at least three authors? In fact, comparisons with earlier versions of themes similar to those in Genesis can be quite as revealing as comparisons of Sophocles' plots with earlier variants of the same myths. There is no better way of finding out what is distinctive in a work.

51

When speaking of the art of reading, I introduced the notion of the philosophical dimension of some texts. The brief account of *the creation of the world and of man* in Genesis clearly has such a dimension. Any reader who merely develops some sense for the style and poetry of the original will be richly rewarded but will still miss much of what these verses are about. Again I can only be highly schematic, suggesting topics that one might attempt to explore in some detail in a course.

Having savored the beauty of the Biblical account, one might proceed to compare it with older versions, which can be found, for example, in *Ancient Near Eastern Texts Relat-*

ing to the Old Testament, edited by James Pritchard. How does the Bible differ from them in style, in content, and in its implications? In what ways was its conception of the world, of man's place in it, and of God and of man's relation to him distinctive?

Next one might deal with parallel or rival versions found outside the Near East. One should contrast the creation of the world and man in Genesis with the accounts of the creation in the Rigveda and in Plato's *Timaeus.* One should also consider ancient Indian attempts to derive the caste system from the way in which men were made from different parts of the primeval man, and Plato's myth in the *Republic,* suggesting that some men have gold in their blood, some silver, and some a baser metal.

Then one might study the impact of the Biblical myth. The notion that all men were descended from a single couple led to the conception that all men are brothers; and the story that man was made in the image of God and that God breathed his spirit into him led to the notion that man, and by no means just some king or priest, was more similar to God than to the other animals. Flatly contradicting what strikes us as the abundant evidence of our senses, man was held to be by no means a mere speck in nature but essentially discontinuous with it and vastly more important. While this conceit—if that is what it is—was carried further here than in India, it is striking, though it has gone practically unnoticed, that in ancient art—and in the West before Dürer—we find not a single landscape painting anywhere. As early as the cave paintings of southern France and northern Spain, we encounter a magnificent feeling for animals, whether or not the interest in them was prompted largely by the hunter's desire for success; but we find no evidence at all in art of any comparable feeling for nature. It was by no means only Genesis that bequeathed to us a stunningly anthropocentric view. What was distinctive in Genesis was the implication that all men are brothers and have a divine dignity.

What little there is of nature in Roman painting, such as ornamental still lifes of edible fruit, does not contradict these claims any more than the tiny trees and mountains that appear in the backgrounds of some of Leonardo's portraits. For the Italian Renaissance a landscape is at most a small decorative background behind persons who seem all-important even if, but for the painting, no one would remember them. Actually, Leonardo, like Dürer, his contemporary, took some interest in natural forms and landscapes and, around 1500, succeeded in rendering them with superb skill in some sketches. But the notion of a vast world of nature in which human beings are exceedingly small or not even to be seen at all was as alien to Leonardo as it was to Michelangelo when he painted the creation on the ceiling of the Sistine Chapel.

In ancient China we find no creation myth, and Fritz Mote has claimed in *Intellectual Foundations of China* (1971) that this is the most distinctive feature of Chinese thought. However that may be, it is in China that we first encounter landscape painting, and in the great scrolls of the Sung dynasty, painted around A.D. 1000, nature is rendered large and people are so small that often it takes quite a while to find them. In the best works of this type we find an economy that invites comparison with Genesis. But the sparseness and simplicity in China and in Israel communicate an altogether different sensibility.

We are now ready to contrast the world views of Western science with Genesis 1 and 2. It was only after Copernicus that Pieter Bruegel the Elder, in the sixteenth century, sometimes placed human beings in landscapes that are decidedly not seen merely as backgrounds. Dürer had done watercolors of pure landscapes a little earlier, and later Rembrandt and Ruisdael did this on a larger scale, in oils. But

on the whole man looms large in Western art, which is in
this respect closer to Genesis than to modern science. Although modern science developed in the West, it is closer in
many ways to Buddhist speculations about many worlds
than it is to Genesis.

Finally, the creation in Genesis should be compared with
the confused common sense of the West in the twentieth
century. This common sense owes a great deal to Genesis
and to modern science, but it tends to be a jumble of incon-
sistencies. One might sort out a few of these before going on
to the tree of the knowledge of good and evil, the expulsion
from paradise, and Cain and Abel.

52

Every one of these stories could be studied along similar
lines. In some cases one might gain an additional dimension
by contrasting a Biblical story with some later literary
treatments of the same theme. Often it could add a great
deal if one showed some slides of paintings that were inspired by the stories and treated the pictures not as mere
illustrations but as interpretations, versions, or developments. Occasionally, musical works might be discussed as
well.

One final example may bring this discussion of Genesis
to a close: the *Akedah,* which is the Hebrew name for the
story told in the first nineteen verses of Genesis 22. Once
again the Latin adage, *multum in parvo,* much in a small
space, is an understatement. A haunting story is told in a
few short sentences, stunning in their succinct felicity.

The tale can stand by itself but is obviously meant to be
read against the background of the preceding chapters. The
beginning of Genesis 12 is relevant, where God tells Abraham to leave his home land to go "to a land that I will
show you. And I will make of you a great nation." This

promise is repeated in various ways, perhaps most poig-
nantly in chapter 15, where Abraham questions God:
"What will you give me, seeing I go hence childless, and
the heir of my house is Eliezer of Damascus?" God tells
him that Eliezer will not be his heir; his own seed will be.
"Look at the heavens and count the stars if you can number
them. And he said to him: So shall your seed be." Yet
Abraham's wife, Sarah, remained childless and eventually
urged Abraham to beget a child with her maid, Hagar. The
story of Hagar and her son Ishmael is interspersed in other
tales. God assures Abraham that Sarah will also bear a son,
"and you shall call his name Isaac; and I will establish my
covenant with him as an everlasting covenant, and with his
seed after him." In the following chapter, 18, the promise
that Sarah will give birth to a son is repeated before God
tells Abraham of his intention to destroy Sodom and
Gomorrah because the people in those cities are so wicked.
Abraham argues with God that he must not destroy the good
with the evil and obtains God's promise to spare Sodom if
there are fifty decent people in it. "And Abraham answered
and said: See, I, being but dust and ashes, have undertaken
to speak to the Lord. Perhaps there are five less than fifty
just men; will you destroy the city for the lack of five?" The
argument continues until God grants that he will not destroy
Sodom if there are ten who are just. This story, too, is
relevant to the *Akedah,* for it shows how the Abraham of
Genesis is very different from the Abraham whom Kierkegaard presents to us in *Fear and Trembling,* the influential book in which he offered his reflections on Genesis 22.

There is much more to these chapters which precede the
Akedah. Every one of them could be made the center of
attention instead of merely being mentioned in passing to
suggest that chapter 22 has a context that enhances it. A
teacher spending a whole term on Genesis would certainly
not wish to make one chapter the focal point of the whole

book, as that would be disastrously misleading. In the present context, however, only one more stroke is needed to complete the background. In chapter 21 Sarah prevails on Abraham to drive away Hagar and Ishmael, which grieved Abraham "because of his son. But God said to him: Do not grieve because of the boy and because of your bondwoman; in all that Sarah has said to you listen to her; for in Isaac your seed shall be called. And also of the son of the bondwoman will I make a nation because he is your seed." All of this adds to the poignancy of the beginning of 22.

"And it was after these things that God tested Abraham and said to him: Abraham. And he said: Here I am. And he said: Take your son, the only one, whom you love, Isaac, and go away to the land of Moriah, and offer him there for a burnt offering on one of the hills that I will show you. And Abraham rose up early in the morning and saddled his ass, and took two of his young men with him, and Isaac his son, and split wood for the burnt offering, and rose, and went to the place of which God had told him. On the third day Abraham raised his eyes and saw the place far off. And Abraham said to his young men: Stay here with the ass, and I and the boy will go there and worship and come back to you. And Abraham took the wood for the burnt offering and laid it upon Isaac his son; and he took the fire in his hand, and a knife; and they went, both of them together."

Not a word is said about Abraham's feelings. There is no need for that because "after these things" related in the preceding chapters any feeling reader "knows" what Abraham feels—or rather feels it himself. The terseness creates the tension, and the themes introduced here reverberate through the rest of Genesis, are taken up in the David stories and in the Gospels, and became central in different ways in the Jewish and Christian experience.

Here is the father's love for his son that remains central in the stories of the fathers, reaching an apotheosis in Jacob's

feelings for Joseph and Benjamin. In the Second Book of
Samuel we encounter this theme again, and David's cry
over his rebellious son who had risen up against him remains unforgettable—provided one knows these stories of
which most students have been ignorant for generations:
"My son Absalom, my son, my son Absalom! Would I had
died for you, Absalom, my son, my son!" (18:33; 19:1 in
the Hebrew)

Jacob and David are the two men brought to life most
lovingly and at the greatest length in the Hebrew Bible, and
both are shown to have suffered most deeply from their
intense love of their children. There is nothing comparable
to this in ancient Indian, Greek, or Chinese literature. It is a
distinctively Jewish theme, introduced in Genesis in the
Abraham story. David's sensibility may have been shaped
by the tales of Abraham, Isaac, and Jacob; certainly the
feelings of Jewish fathers through the centuries were influenced profoundly by these stories and by those of David.
Again and again, life imitated literature.

In Genesis we find no comparable feeling for a
daughter—not even in the story about Dinah, Jacob's
daughter, in chapter 34. The tale of Jephthah's sacrifice of
his daughter in Judges 11 comes closer to the *Akedah* and
should be compared with it.

The Christian idea that "God so loved the world that he
gave his only begotten son," in the Gospel according to
John (3:16), clearly harks back to Genesis 22. When the
Greeks related that Tantalus had killed his children and
served the meat to the gods to see if they could tell the
difference from their usual fare, it did not occur to them that
this might have involved any sacrifice on his part; and when
Laius gave orders to let his newborn son, Oedipus, die of
exposure, that was not believed to have involved any suffering for the father who was presumed to have forgotten the
whole matter. The notion that no sacrifice could be greater

than giving one's only son was derived from Genesis and resounds through David's cry.

Even the image of Isaac carrying the wood on which he is to be sacrificed is taken up in the Gospels, where Jesus is said to have carried the cross on which he was to be crucified. Yet in Genesis the story culminates in God's rejection of the notion that the sacrifice of one's son should be required or accepted as a sign of ultimate devotion.

The sacrifice of the firstborn was an ancient custom in that part of the world and not by any means confined to one's children. In Genesis this ancient rite is, in effect, reinterpreted. The sacrifice of the firstborn son becomes the sacrifice of "your son, the only one, whom you love, Isaac"; and the whole emphasis is made to fall not on his being firstborn, which in a sense he is not, but on the father's deep love for him. And then God forbids the sacrifice, commanding Abraham to sacrifice a ram instead.

If this story stood alone, one might still suppose that perhaps the sacrifice was prohibited only in this special case. But Moses and the prophets brand this custom as a heathen rite that is an abomination. It is doubly remarkable that in the New Testament this rite is brought back as an indispensable condition of salvation. No man can be saved if he refuses to believe that God showed his love of man by sacrificing "his only begotten son that whoever believes in him should not perish but have everlasting life" (John 3:16).

One may also think of Isaac walking beside his father when one reads Isaiah's vastly influential description of the man "despised and rejected" who "has borne our griefs and carried our sorrows"—at least when one comes to the line, quoted in the New Testament: "he is brought as a lamb to the slaughter" (53:7). But Isaiah says twice in the same verse that he did not open his mouth, while the author of the story in Genesis lets Isaac speak as he walks with Abraham.

In a perceptive essay on the narrative art of the Bible, H. Steinthal, cofounder with Moritz Lazarus of *Völkerpsychologie* (the psychology of peoples), remarked in the mid-nineteenth century that it might be fruitful to imagine a contest in which the greatest writers of all time vied with each other to invent a fitting dialogue for Abraham and Isaac, picking up the story at the point where we broke off. Steinthal suggested plausibly that none could have improved on Genesis; and we might add that certainly Euripides did not when he dealt with a similar theme in *Iphigenia in Aulis*. What makes the solution in Genesis unsurpassable is once again the terseness that saves it from sentimentality.

"... and they went, both of them together. And Isaac spoke to Abraham, his father, and said: My father. And he said: Here I am, my son. And he said: Here is the fire and the wood; but where is the lamb for a burnt offering? And Abraham said: God will provide himself a lamb for a burnt offering, my son. So they went, both of them together."

Few dialogues in world literature match the pathos of these lines; none their economy. Almost every single word carries an immense weight, yet there are no big or fancy words.

"And they came to the place of which God had told him, and Abraham built an altar there, and laid out the wood, and bound Isaac, his son, and laid him on the altar on the wood. And Abraham stretched out his hand and took the knife to slay his son. And an angel of the Lord called to him out of heaven and said: Abraham! Abraham! And he said: Here I am. And he said: Lay not your hand upon the boy nor do anything to him. . . ."

Akedah means binding, and in Hebrew the whole story is named after that. There is no need here to continue with the rest of the story. I have merely tried to give some idea of its dimensions, and of the sort of thing one might do in a course on Genesis. No doubt, one would also have to point out that, according to Jewish tradition, the place of the Akedah was the rock over which King Solomon later built the first temple, in the early tenth century B.C.—the rock still to be seen inside the Dome of the Rock in Jerusalem.

From here one might easily go on to some discussion of the meaning of this site and of Jerusalem in general for Jews, Christians, and Muslims, paying particular attention to the relation of texts in scriptures to holy sites. For scripture is by definition not mere literature but an authoritative element in a religion. Even when one teaches scripture without claiming authority either for the text or for one's own interpretations, one should not ignore this dimension of its influence and of the meaning it has had for generations of believers.

At the same time, one should rescue the text from being read as a mere relic—as part of a religion that the reader does not share and that perhaps he does not greatly like. Even when one cannot do this with every text, one should try sometimes to show how a text might impinge on the experience of an unbelieving reader *now*. So far from preventing culture shock, the idea would be to heighten the challenge of the text by showing how a modern reader might be haunted by it.

The *Akedah* is a theme that recurs in different ways in some of my own poems—all of them very brief—and if I taught a course on Genesis I should not hesitate to read these poems to show how one reader occasionally returns to the same story and experiences it in a variety of contexts, including an encounter with the *Akedah* in a Muslim country. It would make sense to look for short poems by various hands to supply additional perspectives on this and other texts.

It would also be instructive to compare the ancient Jewish

mosaic of the *Akedah* in the synagogue of Bet Alpha in Israel with later Christian mosaics. The story is also illustrated in medieval Hebrew Bibles and prayer books, and the early Christians dealt with it in paint, glass, and ivory. Major Italian artists who took up this theme include Ghiberti, Donatello, Andrea del Sarto, Sodoma, Titian, Caravaggio, Guardi, and Tiepolo. Ghiberti's two bronze doors at the Baptistery in Florence are world-famous. The one completed first is adorned with scenes from the New Testament, the second door presents Old Testament themes and is known as the Gates of Paradise—a tribute first paid to Ghiberti's artistry by Michelangelo. It is less well known that each of the seven artists who competed for the original assignment had to do a bronze *Akedah*. Ghiberti won, and his version and that of the runner-up, Brunelleschi, who later built the dome of the cathedral of Florence, are now in the Bargello in Florence. Rembrandt treated the story in an etching and a famous painting. And in our time, Igor Stravinsky composed *Akedat Yizhak,* a ballad for baritone and chamber orchestra set to a Hebrew text.

53

A scholar is almost bound to ask at this point, if not long before, whether any course of this kind could possibly be respectable. Religion, he might feel, is one thing, but this is too much, involving work that ought to be done properly in many different departments. In fact, however, religion is not one thing that can be studied alongside other departments that preempt literature, art, music, philosophy, and history. The place of religion in higher education is not least of all to remind us of the artificiality of our departmental boundaries.

A scholar might respond, reasonably, that in bygone

times religion did indeed permeate the lives of people, notably their art and literature, philosophy and music and, alas,
their history—for example, in the age of the Crusades—but
that academic progress, not only in science, has been due to
our success in setting boundaries not only for religion but
for other subjects, too. To make progress, he might say, we
have to stick to one discipline in which we have attained
some competence. Anything else is likely to be amateurish
and a bad example for our students.

These are half-truths, and it is important to see what is
right in all this. But where would this leave us when it
comes to teaching Genesis? Or Buddhism? Buddhism is not
only literature but also Angkor Thom in Cambodia and
Borobodur in Java, Thai bronzes and Japanese statues
carved from wood, people pouring water over gilded images
on the great terrace of the Shwe Dagon pagoda in Rangoon
and palmistry in Mandalay; the emperor Ashoka and the
caves at Ajanta as well as Zen and the art of swordsman-
ship. Any notion that religion is mainly theology is a be-
trayal of man. Religion is far too important to be left to
theologians.

It is easy to read a religious text—Genesis is merely an
example—many times until one knows it well after a fashion and is even ready to pass examinations on it, and still to
have very little sense of its significance. To understand that,
one simply has to make comparisons with other texts, including some written in different cultures, and one has to
trace at least some of its influence in art and literature,
beginning with later parts of the Hebrew Bible and the Gospels and including Michelangelo's interpretations. To do all
that is far from easy and in fact quite apt to be done badly.
But much teaching is bad anyway, and the mere fact that a
subject might be taught ineptly is not a sufficient reason for
not teaching it at all.

Religion ought to be taught well at the level of higher

education, and the way to do it well has to be interdisciplinary. That raises a general point about higher education, which needs to be considered at some length. An interdisciplinary approach is dangerous, but so is everything in life that is most worthwhile, including love.

CHAPTER FIVE:
VISION CAN
BE
TAUGHT, BUT...

54

Blindness can be taught, and has been taught for centuries. A great deal of education has always been indoctrination. Students were taught what to believe and exhorted not to see inconvenient facts, alternatives, or even their own beliefs. Piety consisted in staying inside, in the dark, believing what you were told. To see for yourself or go outside to find out how your beliefs looked when you stepped back far enough to see them was impiety.

   Luther, who relished bluntness, insisted that you have to tear the eyes out of your reason; else you could in no way enter the kingdom of heaven. Others, though equally dogmatic, have not said so openly that they were making a virtue of blindness. They preferred to stress how important reason was—as a handmaid of faith. In this respect Marxism is closer to Roman Catholicism than it is to Luther.

These considerations do not apply only to religion and to ideologies that are embraced by millions as substitute religions. To some extent they apply to every scholasticism. The consensus of the school takes the place of a religious or political faith. Here we are far removed from Luther's dictum; the typical modern scholastic is so blind that, unlike Luther, he cannot see what he is doing. He is not aware of having any sacrosanct beliefs that he never questions and refuses to look at. Even if he says "we" often—not counting the harmless editorial "we" of phrases like "we have seen"—he never gives himself an account of the beliefs that make up the consensus to which he appeals. More often than not, he will deny that he belongs to a school, and the very suggestion that the consensus on which he bases himself defines one school among many has not occurred to him and, if pressed on him, is resented and quickly forgotten. He cannot see his own beliefs, his own position, or his own condition; and to talk to him about it and tell him that he is blind would be very indelicate.

Being subtle to a fault, how can he fail to see that he belongs to one school among others? This is so odd that one might simply refuse to believe it if the academic world were not full of such cases. The typical modern scholastic equates his school of thought with what reasonable men believe and admits that many people in his field are not reasonable or have been taught badly or are members of departments of which everybody knows that they are below par.

This feat could hardly be brought off without a drug. The scholastic's panacea, which serves simultaneously as a tranquilizer, painkiller, and stimulant, is hyperspecialization. Taken in large quantities, it has the same effect as wood alcohol; it makes one blind.

Blindness is also taught in a much more obvious way, at a

lower level. Children who enter school full of imagination and ideas are squelched by uncreative, anticreative disciplinarians. The solution to all these problems would be very simple if one could teach vision by doing away with discipline and specialization, and perhaps even with schools. This "cure," however, is worse than the condition that it seeks to remedy.

This comparison can be made easily because this simple-minded quackery leaves people blind and in addition leads to either slavery or chaos. We cannot dispense with specialization, much less with schools. *Vision can be taught to some extent, but not by those who are afraid of discipline or of thinking about goals.*

We shall consider discipline first, then the liberal arts education that stresses the humanities and is the one kind of higher education that may seem not to be goal-directed, and then the longstanding refusal of teachers and students to think about goals, during both the age of the teacups and the age of specialization that followed it. Finally, I shall discuss what I take to be the four major reasons for teaching the humanities, and one of these is to teach vision.

55

Many people hate and resent discipline and would like to be free to play; but the games they enjoy playing and watching have complicated rules that one may not violate. At the very least, even small transgressions entail penalties; often they mean that one has lost the game or even that one may not play again. The rules define the game, and the satisfaction one derives from it depends on rigorous discipline. The popular notion that discipline and play represent basic alternatives is untenable.

The fact that play is fun proves that discipline can be enjoyable. A lack of structure, a situation in which anything goes, is experienced as threatening when it lasts; and the threat can be specified. One feels menaced by the loss of meaning, by the lack of any purpose. A game has a purpose, which is generally to win; and whenever that becomes too easy, the game is quickly felt to be pointless and boring. It is no fun anymore.

The idea that children may learn things through play makes good sense. What is silly is the conceit that play can dispense with discipline. Without discipline man faces despair.

This is not to say that vision spells despair and that only blindness can save us. On the contrary, we have already seen in the discussion of "Four Kinds of Minds" how visionaries need discipline, and before long we shall return to this theme.

The idea that discipline is merely the price we have to pay for living with others is wrong. Nowhere does a human being need it more than in solitary confinement if he does not want to go out of his mind.

It does not follow that the needed discipline must be imposed from outside, much less than this or that specific code of rules is needed. The rules of games are for the most part obviously arbitrary, yet we should not be better off if we abolished them. Games depend on having rules, and a proposal to change a rule of a game makes no sense unless it is based on more than the truism that the old rule is arbitrary.

If the case is different in education, that is because education is not merely a game. The aim is not merely to pass the time in a way that is felt to be enjoyable. Nor is the goal merely to win in a competition. There is more of this playful element even in *higher* education and in the rarefied regions of research where Nobel prizes are won than most people ever realized until James Watson's *The Double Helix* (1968) called attention to these matters. There is a delight in cracking a code or advancing difficult problems toward solutions. But if that were all, we should need very stringent rules, as in doing puzzles, chess, or bridge, and students' protests that the rules were arbitrary would not carry any weight at all. The case for criticizing all sorts of requirements depends on the assumption, which happens to be right, that education from the first grade to the most advanced research is always directed toward goals, even if few people are very clear about these.

Prominent among the first goals are the abilities to read and write, add and subtract, divide and multiply. These are skills that virtually everybody could be taught by the age of eight or at most ten, but many people have deep doubts whether it is really important for *everyone* to be able to spell or to write his native language clearly and grammatically. Such questions are worth asking but become pernicious when it is maintained at the same time that everybody ought to go to school and perhaps even to college. Those who insist on that while questioning or denying outright the need for students to learn basic skills deprive the schools of meaning and make them breeding grounds of resentment and despair.

For school must involve a lot of discipline. Bringing together large numbers of children in a few rooms, with one teacher in each room, means chaos and universal dissatisfaction unless there is discipline. And if there is discipline and order is preserved, but there is nothing to be won, the children, like the teachers, quickly come to feel that the whole game is pointless.

Only the possibility of triumphs can redeem school. To speak of triumphs over ignorance would be mere rhetoric, remote from concrete experience. But to be able to read a word, a sentence, a page, a story, a whole book, are triumphs. To be able to write, to send a letter, to solve various problems, or to understand what people say when they speak a foreign language—these are triumphs, too. Of course, writing a letter and thus being able to communicate with someone far away is much less thrilling in the telephone age than it used to be, and the art of writing is deteriorating. School, however, can be redeemed only by learning, and learning cannot be divorced from discipline and should not be divorced from the thrill of triumph.

56

Those who question whether there is any need for *everyone* to learn to read and write and master other basic skills should weigh the consequences of a bifurcation of society in which some would be literate and others not. Historically, almost all societies have always been divided like that, and many still are. The notion that this is bad and that a whole society could be literate comes from Sinai.

No sooner had Israel arrived at Mount Sinai than "Moses went up to God, and the Lord called to him out of the mountain, saying: Thus shall you say to the house of Jacob and tell the children of Israel: . . . You shall be unto me a kingdom of priests. . . ." These words precede even the Ten Commandments, which are given in the following chapter, Exodus 20. Until then few but priests had been literate in the Near East. In India only the Brahmins knew the sacred lore, and there is no evidence that even they possessed the arts of reading and writing before the third century B.C. We have written records from the Indus Valley culture that came to an end in the sixteenth century B.C., before the Aryan invasion, and then again from the period of Ashoka, after Alexander's invasion, but none at all from the intervening thirteen centuries. Nor is there any mention of writing or writing utensils in the voluminous literature of the Vedas and Upanishads or in the earliest Buddhist literature. There is every reason to believe that all this literature was transmitted orally for centuries, and this hypothesis helps us to understand the esoteric tradition in Hinduism as well as the style of the Buddha's sermons. In the Hebrew Bible, on the other hand, writing is mentioned constantly, and the Jews have been almost totally literate for going on three thousand years. The Christian world set aside the commandment to become a kingdom of priests, which seemed to be so patently addressed to the Jews only—until Luther recalled it in his battle against the Roman clergy, insisting again and again that all men are called to be priests.

The invention of the art of printing, made in Germany thirty years before Luther's birth, was a decisive turning point. It enabled Luther to place his new German translation of the Bible in every German Protestant household, and soon literacy flourished in the Protestant world as it never had in the Roman Catholic or the Orthodox realm. Luther was anything but a democrat, but the rapid spread of literacy in northern Europe, notably including France as well as England, precipitated the enlightenment and the development of democratic theories. There is clearly a close connection, by no means only historical, between literacy and education on the one hand and civil rights and participation in government on the other.

The reasons for giving a primary education to *all* are largely social. They depend on the kind of society we want to have. Whoever desires to maintain a caste society in which some groups can never rise above the level of outcastes has excellent reasons for opposing universal literacy.

The wish to preserve the highly privileged position and almost unchecked power of a small minority might also lead one to oppose education for the masses. On the other hand, this minority might realize that such a policy would lead to technological backwardness and quite possibly starvation and other unwelcome results and that, again for social reasons, a large pool of educated talent was required. Those who believe in any form or fashion that all human beings are made in God's image—and the so-called theory of natural rights is little more than a well-intentioned but implausible way of saying this without mentioning God—may prefer to plead for universal education *without* speaking of the social consequences.

In any case, nearly universal literacy is not sufficient to protect a society against tyranny, as Hitler showed. But the social consequences of having two large groups in a society, one literate and one not, are plain. When this division is hereditary and coincides with a difference in color, it is doubly pernicious. Anyone who wishes to eliminate discrimination against groups of people according to their color or religion must make sure that such groups are not for the most part much less literate and far more unskilled than most of the rest of the population.

57

In the end one has to educate oneself—but most students must first learn how to do this. Without the help of parents or older friends, only the most strong-willed and self-disciplined can manage without teachers, and there are not enough teachers for everyone to have private tutors. Hence schools are needed to teach basic skills, including the self-discipline one needs to educate oneself. Schools should also expose students to the joys of learning, the thrill of discovery and triumph, and the close connection between discipline and the delights of mastery.

In many fields a lot of discipline at a very early age is invaluable. Starting from scratch at the age of eighteen, one does not have a chance to become a great composer or a good violinist or pianist, or a great chess master or mathematician, or a fine scholar. Most scholars nowadays are worse scholars for not having learned more languages before and during adolescence. Moreover, the mind, and in some cases also the body, has to be disciplined early.

It is very well to tell children how wonderful their drawings are, and for fond parents to feel as much pleasure in their children's work as in a Leonardo. But the children will soon cease to get much satisfaction from their work if they do not feel that in some sense they are making progress and can point to an occasional triumph. Leonardo's teacher, Verrocchio, whose statue of Bartolomeo Colleoni on horseback is one of the greatest sculptures of all time, was not a "progressive" teacher who felt that any work was as good as any other.

Leonardo and Michelangelo were by no means strangers to despair. But they took enormous pride in their creations, working very hard at them, and deriving comfort from their work. The requisite self-discipline was acquired through years of disciplined study. In the end, both excelled in *many* disciplines. It is far easier for one who has gained mastery in one discipline to also master two or three others than it is for a person without discipline to learn to master one.

58

Once goals are specified, rules and requirements are open to criticism if they are counterproductive or not functional. Both a critique and a defense have to appeal to goals, although the goals themselves can be questioned, too. Self-discipline is an especially important primary goal, meaning that it is not an end in itself but needed for the achievement of other ends. Some of these could be called ends in themselves. Without self-discipline there is no mastery of any kind, nor autonomy, nor creativity that keeps on yielding satisfaction. Self-discipline is not enough, but those who lack it head for slavery or despair, or both.

The only way to learn self-discipline is through first being disciplined by others, and insofar as discipline imposed from outside does succeed in teaching one self-discipline it serves a purpose, although it makes sense to ask if the same aim could not also be attained at much less cost by a less brutal regimen. When discipline is so harsh that it snuffs out creativity and independence instead of building up self-confidence, it is counterproductive and a crime against the spirit.

It is no accident that in several languages "discipline" also means a branch of learning. Both meanings of the word are derived from a Latin word for learning. Learning involves discipline in many ways. One of these is that we must not keep running off in different directions, trying something only for a minute before we take up something else for a few seconds, and then something else again. We have to concentrate on one thing at a time and persevere even when we feel discouraged. This is true even of basic skills like reading, writing, and arithmetic, or learning how to ride a bicycle or drive a car.

The case for learning one thing well after we have mastered a number of basic skills is worth spelling out. To be good at something and hence able to take pride in our work gives us a measure of self-confidence that is needed for constructive humility and self-criticism. It should also provide us with a means of self-support and a basis for acquiring further skills and mastering more disciplines. Self-support is important not for its own sake but as a condition of independence and autonomy; and if one can foresee that even being very good at something is not at all likely to become a means of self-support, this is reason enough for seriously considering other careers. With a firm base somewhere, we can still hope to cultivate our first love, too. In scholarship monogamy is not a virtue. And to choose a career in which one is doomed to failure, for whatever reason, is stupid and does no one any good.

59

At every level education should be goal-directed. In the early years, the goal should be mastery of basic skills, including the self-discipline required for meaningful work and satisfaction in any field. Other basic skills are reading well, writing clearly, some mathematics, some geography and history, a little science, and a foreign language. All this is familiar but not quite enough. Students should also learn a little about medicine in secondary school, first aid, and—in societies in which cars are common—how to drive *well*.

The aims of graduate schools are also easier to formulate than those of colleges. A society must give some thought to its needs, and it should make every effort to assure a sufficient supply of doctors and lawyers, teachers and engineers, chemists and physicists, as well as pilots, farmers, pharmacists, and electricians. This is not an argument for regimentation, but when a country turns out within a few years more than two thousand Ph.D.'s in philosophy alone who cannot find jobs, this is a serious failure. And when with an unprecedented college population and unexcelled facilities for the study of medicine it produces during those same years so few physicians that most hospitals have to employ doctors from Asian countries where they are needed desperately, this is tragic. In such circumstances, medical schools should admit more students—whether the American Medical Association likes it or not—and graduate programs in the humanities fewer students; and we should advertise our needs and tell young people plainly what their prospects for employment are in various fields. This information ought to be available to all interested students even before they enter college.

Of course, not all goals are vocational. It is arguable that a college education should not be designed primarily to prepare students for graduate school but rather to prepare them for their leisure hours. But that is not to say that

college education can dispense with goals. In the prologue I
have stated briefly what I take to be the major goals of the
humanities, and soon I shall return to this theme.

60

The liberal arts college is a blessed anomaly. An education
in the humanities does not have any obvious purpose, and
yet there are many people who insist that it is vitally
important for everyone to go to such a college. There is a
vague sense that the years spent in such a school are apt to
be the best time of one's life, and that something that is so
good should not be a privilege reserved for the few.

In a way a good liberal arts college *is* an isle of the
blessed in a cruel world. I can think of no better way of
showing this than to recall my own experience of coming to
such a college early in 1939. I had left Nazi Germany,
crossed the Atlantic in a hurricane, and suddenly found
myself in an altogether different world. In ever so many
tangible ways, I encountered freedom. The students could
pursue their intellectual interests, and the professors could
do the same, criticizing any view they pleased. It would
have been boorish to ask about the purpose of all this; it was
so beautiful. Actually, my own goal was clear. I had wanted
to enter a professional school but was not admitted without a
college degree; and my purpose was to get that as quickly as
I could. But the requirement struck me as stupid. Having
graduated from a German secondary school, a so-called
Gymnasium, in the spring of 1938, I could have entered a
university and obtained a doctorate in three years, had it not
been for Hitler. Now I was required to spend two and a half
years on getting a B.A. before I could commence graduate
work in 1941.

In March 1939 it looked as if war might break out; in
September World War II began, but the United States did

not enter the war until six months after my graduation. What struck me was the stunning independence of the school, which in some respects might almost as well have been on the moon. Of course, some political science courses were popular, especially those of a professor who was an eloquent interventionist. A great variety of points of view was represented on the faculty and also at conferences attended by prominent scholars and politicians from outside. Many of the most popular and respected professors were in humanities departments; the war in which some of my classmates were to die was more than three thousand miles away; Japan was even much more remote; and in those days there were no passenger flights across the oceans, and the American liberal arts colleges did not seem to be in the same world with Europe and Asia. Nor was it fashionable to ask about their purpose.

At one time the rationale of such colleges was to turn boys into gentlemen who would know how to hold a teacup and to conduct polite and civilized conversations during the abundant hours of their leisure. The whole idea in those days was *not* to specialize. At Oxford one learned Latin and Greek for no special purpose, even as one learned to speak with an Oxford accent for no reason in particular. The idea was to speak as people who had not had similar advantages did not speak, and to learn languages and a few other things that they did not know. To be civilized meant to be different and superior, and those who had enjoyed this kind of education were considered fit to run the country or a business without knowing economics or having any other clearly relevant skills. Few became dons; fewer still, scholars.

In the United States there was also some concern for providing a preliminary education for young men who wanted to become parsons. But the most prestigious colleges were the least goal-oriented and the most expensive, and before World War II few but the wealthy could afford to go to them, nor was there any presumption that after graduation most students would go on to learn some vocation. On the contrary, it was assumed that a high percentage would go into business, usually their fathers', having learned nothing that could be expected to be useful to them. Some, of course, would go to medical or law school, but again the idea was to give them some general education first. The very notion of utility seemed Philistine.

It was in those days that it was considered admirable for a teacher to be Socratic, and there was also some loose talk about the unexamined life not being worth living. But it was difficult to find professors who ran any risk of ever being accused of impiety, as Socrates was. One was genteel and did not think of questioning the faith and morals of one's society—at least not in one's own way, without the support of any rival creed or ideology, like Socrates.

For those who went to school during those years it is not difficult to idealize that time. It is no more difficult to ridicule it. During the age of the teacups there was no slogan "Publish or perish!" A young academic was supposed to have nice manners, and it was sometimes claimed that one's behavior at teas proved crucial when decisions on promotions were made. It was only World War II that brought to an end the age of the teacups.

Actually, the change in the climate was not sudden, and during the Eisenhower years the atmosphere at American colleges was still very genteel. Ike said that he did not care what faith a man had as long as he had a faith; students admired Kierkegaard for speaking of "subjective truth"; they liked to say that "this is true for me" while something else might well be "true for you"; and professors for the most part had no inkling of the genuine Socratic ethos.

61

What eventually replaced the age of the teacups was the age of specialization. It may be ungracious to speak of an age of teacups, but it is important to grasp the limitations of the age that preceded the age of specialization, especially if one is highly critical of certain aspects of the later age. After all, in some ways the change was clearly for the better.

In fact, it is easy to find *reasons* why specialization is needful and why anything short of it is amateurish and reprehensible; but the arrival of the new age was not based on arguments, much less on proofs. The change was a historical development that had *causes*.

Some of the causes have been noted in the first chapter. The main cause was the rapid expansion of the college population after World War II. Wealth was no longer a prerequisite for getting into college. In the United States veterans were entitled to a college education, and more and more scholarships were made available for nonveterans as well. Unprecedented numbers of students applied for admission, and while unprecedented numbers were admitted and many new schools were founded, also in other countries, most schools tried to *select* their students, making use of competitive examinations; and quickly the whole educational system changed. Masses of new teachers were needed, and faculty hiring and promotions suddenly involved far larger numbers of people than ever before. At every level quantitative measurements were needed to facilitate quick evaluations of quantities of people. Hence examinations and publications became ever more important.

Until then, the majority of the students admitted to the most prestigious colleges and universities in England and in the United States had been prepared at schools that were very expensive and in many ways resembled the colleges. Now it was felt that students who had not attended such exclusive schools should have an equal chance, and tests were introduced to provide some objective measure of ability. Whatever was wrong with many of the tests, the *intention* was decent and humane. Some applicants come from exclusive schools and are highly recommended by a head-master known to the director of admissions, while other applicants come from unknown schools. Grades furnish no reliable clue if one does not know the standards of the teachers. If one relies solely on interviews to sort out the applicants, the prejudices of the interviewers may vitiate the selection, and in any case it does not seem to be a good idea to let everything depend on a brief conversation. The reason for introducing tests was to have a more objective measure in addition to the interviews and letters.

Essay questions pose two crucial problems. It takes very long to read thousands of answers, and different readers may evaluate the answers very differently. Hence it was decided to develop multiple-choice tests. In the humanities such tests are nevertheless very problematic. A certain amount of information can be tested in this way; but as soon as the questions become a bit subtler, tests of this sort favor the scholastic who thrives on consensus while they penalize the visionary and Socratic types.

If we assume that these types have not crystallized at the age when such tests are taken, it is still important that such tests serve notice that what is desired is scholasticism. Those with a vision of their own or, more simply, students with some originality are not favored by such tests; and the Socratically inclined who love to question the consensus and who look with a critical eye at the questions and the four answers of which one and only one is supposed to be right learn that this posture does not pay. More important still, more and more secondary school teachers precisely at the best schools in which many students want to go on to a good college began to prepare their students for these tests. Students who were not used to such tests were at a great disadvantage; students whose education had been designed to prepare them for these tests had been trained not to be Socratic or original.

During the same period the graduate schools gained an importance they had never had before. As masses of new teachers were needed, graduate schools doubled and trebled their enrollments, and departments and whole colleges that had never had graduate programs suddenly developed them. Money was made available for this purpose by the administration and by various levels of the government. To get hold of one's "share" of these funds, one had to develop such a program. Not to have a graduate program became a sign of lack of enterprise and lack of distinction, and to attract graduate students and set an example for them one had to do research and publish articles in scholarly journals. In looking for teachers, one looked for people who would do that; and those who did not publish were not kept on when their probationary period had expired. At the same time, the undergraduate college curriculum came to be conceived more and more as the necessary preparation for graduate study.

Finally, Sputnik—the first Russian spacecraft, launched in October 1957—proved to be a crucial factor in the transformation of education. The prestige of the natural sciences had been very great for a long time. Educated people had long been conscious of the enormous progress made in the sciences for more than a century. This progress was actually accelerating. Positivism had become prominent in the nineteenth century and had spread during the first half of the twentieth century. Its central faith was, in a nutshell, that progress in all academic disciplines, including the humanities, depended on emulation of the natural sciences. Even so, undergraduate education in the English-speaking world had remained to a remarkable degree in the age of the teacups. In philosophy, for example, positivism took the form of what was sometimes called ordinary language philosophy or Oxford philosophy (although it had begun at Cambridge University in England), and for all its bombast

about a revolution in philosophy and its disparagement of
"amateurs" and of what one might think up some afternoon
in one's armchair, this was straight teacups philosophy—a
pleasant game for amateurs who lacked specialized knowledge of anything in particular but took pride in knowing
what one could say and what would sound "very odd." In a
way, it was a matter of knowing what was "U" (upper class
and respectable) and what was "non-U." This did allow for
clear distinctions among students as well as teachers, depending on how clever a chap was and how well he played
this game. As numbers increased, so did the importance of
being able to make such distinctions. But if anyone asked
what the point of some celebrated article might be, he was
either put in his place with some such remark as "I should
have thought that that was rather obvious," or he was
treated, rather more appropriately, like someone who had
asked what was the point of playing chess or bridge, or of
holding a teacup nicely and having good manners.

Sputnik did not smash the teacups all at once. But the
American government became alarmed that the Russian
Communists were suddenly ahead of the United States and
"the free world." A crash program was needed to ensure
that America would be first. This involved not only a space
program but also very massive outlays to upgrade higher
education. The central intent was to aid the sciences and
engineering, but it did not prove feasible to introduce a
blatant caste system into the colleges and universities, paying the scientists at an altogether different rate. Professors in
all fields benefited but knew that what was really esteemed
was science. This helped still further to speed the emulation
of the sciences and the contempt for anything unscientific.
Thus specialization received yet another great boost.

In the United States, the establishment of the National
Science Foundation and the decision of the Department of
Defense to make research grants to professors gave an

added impetus to these tendencies. Not only did the scientists who received grants gain further income and prestige, but professors in the humanities, notably in philosophy, soon discovered that they, too, could win grants from the N.S.F. or the D.o.D. if they presented projects that looked scientific rather than humanistic. As a result many of the brightest and most enterprising younger scholars were lost to the humanities.

It was still all right to be a Socratic type if one was content to teach undergraduates at a college that did not have any graduate program and if one did not care for prestige, grants, or leaves of absence. Those who did research in the *humanities* could not hope for a secretary of their own or a regular summer stipend of two-ninths of their annual salary.

Anyone with too large a specialty was obviously resigned to never making any serious contribution. Eighteenth-century French literature and Renaissance art obviously were too large to be respectable specialties. Nietzsche had recognized this even in the 1880s when in the last part of *Zarathustra* he made fun of the conscientious scholar who exclaimed that the leech would be far too vast a field for him and that his specialty was the brain of the leech.

62

It is as easy to make fun of the age of specialization and to produce ridiculous examples from the humanities as it is to explain and defend the rationale of the system. The easiest way to do both is to refer to the seed of the whole system, the doctoral dissertation.

With no trouble at all, one could fill a page with grotesque titles of Ph.D. theses in the humanities. Nor would this be unfair, for these essays are supposed to be contributions to knowledge, and by writing them students make the transition to scholarship and teaching. Anyone writing a few more pieces of a similar nature is generally considered fit to be advanced to a professorship.

On the other hand, suppose a student comes to you with the request that you should supervise his dissertation, which will be a two-volume work on German philosophy since Kant. In that case you do not merely tell him that one volume is more than enough, you also insist on a much smaller topic. Why? For several reasons. The project lacks a focus, and even if it had one it would still take much too long to do a good job. A thesis is a requirement that one should get out of the way in a year if at all possible so that one can cease being a graduate student and become self-supporting. It is a way of demonstrating that one can think and write clearly, that one has learned how to do research, and that one can organize one's materials. One should also demonstrate some awareness of the literature as well as the ability to deal critically with views one rejects. In sum, it is meant as a test of certain basic skills, and all such tests should be got out of the way at an early age. Once that is done, one can hope for a more nearly autonomous position—for example, as a teacher and a scholar who no longer needs a professor's consent before he embarks on a project. Hence the proper subject for a thesis will almost always be relatively small. In philosophy, it could hardly be a whole century or even a whole philosopher but perhaps one of the theories of a philosopher—at which point we are no longer so far from the brain of the leech.

It does not follow that a dissertation must, or should, be trivial. The theory in question does not have to be of purely antiquarian interest. It could be a theory that has been largely ignored or generally misunderstood although, when interpreted correctly, it is fruitful and an interesting alternative to a prevalent doctrine. Or a reinterpretation of this theory may place a philosopher who has become the subject of a large secondary literature in a new light.

Of course, a thesis in the history of philosophy does not

have to concentrate on one philosopher. I once suggested to a student that he write his dissertation on alienation, examining the many different uses to which this term had been put by Hegel, Marx, and some of their successors, and pointing up some of the major confusions that had been, and still were, associated with it. After he got his doctorate, he put a lot more work into his thesis, and eventually it was published as a book, not only in hard covers but also as a paperback that reached a wide audience.

A thesis in the humanities does not have to be historical. It could be an attempt to work out a theory of one's own, or a critique of some widely held view, or an analysis of a play, of a work of art, or of a religious concept. In every case, however, a student should master the literature on his subject, show an awareness of the major views that have been held, and deal critically with some of the major alternatives. In that way he becomes something of a specialist.

63

In a scholastic environment, the range of alternatives that are seriously considered will usually be quite narrow. The professor who supervises the student's work gives him a reading list or at least suggests orally what is worth reading, and what is not. As a rule, approaches that are utterly at variance with the supervisor's are ignored. The student is given to understand that he should not waste his time on literature of that sort. He is taught to blind himself.

Having done that, he is not likely to recover his vision later on. But it does not follow that specialization *must* be deleterious. The student could be taught to go out of his way to look for radical alternatives and to consider possible objections to his own approach and views. He could be told that looking at the literature on his subject is a means to this end. If so, he will also become a specialist who knows his subject and the literature on it pretty thoroughly; but his thesis will be the proving ground where he acquires some of the habits that facilitate vision.

Dissertations are important, although few indeed are memorable. It is usually a waste of time to read a doctor's thesis, but even when that is the case it was not necessarily a waste of time to write it. What makes dissertations important is that they set a pattern for the years to come. It is at this point that the final damage is often done; but a thesis can also become the apprentice piece of a master.

Here the ways part. Some realize that *specialization is an indispensable propaedeutic*. Others go on to specialize more and more to become great experts on something so small and often trivial that nobody except a few other pedants in the same boat would ever like to hear about it. That is the direction in which the humanities have moved since the fifties, and they did not start from scratch even then.

Professors with small specialties have not only insisted more and more on teaching their work in progress to their students but have also tried to hire colleagues who shared their interests, with the result that their students were reared on a highly specialized diet. Whole departments at leading universities have based their claims on excellence on the boast that nobody could equal their collection of experts on the brain of the leech.

As long as there were ample fellowships for students who wished to study the same area or to pursue the same approach, and the professors could see to it that the fellowships went to those who, for whatever reasons, had this interest, and there were jobs with good pay for such hyperspecialists, no arguments about vision, autonomy, or purposes carried any weight. Money talks, in academia, too.

An economic crisis, like any other crisis, can become a blessing if it leads to some reflection on goals. The sudden evaporation of fellowship funds and jobs need not be an unmitigated disaster. The human cost is high but need not be for nothing. It takes extreme situations to open people's eyes and make them think about ends.

64

First of all, we should think about our own goals. Human beings have a deep reluctance to do this. This phenomenon I have discussed in detail in *Without Guilt and Justice: From Decidophobia to Autonomy*. Decidophobia is what I call the fear of fateful decisions. Any serious reflection on our goals in life involves consideration of alternatives and requires fateful decisions.

For roughly twenty years, from about 1950 until 1970, large numbers of students entered graduate schools and then went on to teach philosophy or history or religion, literature or art, without ever having seriously reflected on their goals. Going into graduate work was rarely experienced as a fateful plunge; on the contrary, it meant staying in school for a few more years—a prolongation of the status quo. One did not even choose where to go; one applied to at least half a dozen schools without knowing very much about any of them, taking the advice of some professors about where one should apply, and feeling all the while that filling out a lot of forms for six or more schools did not involve any frightening decision; and if more than one school sent a letter of acceptance, many students went to the one that offered the largest fellowship.

Few gave any thought to the obvious fact that the humanities are not useful in the same immediate way in which medicine and other professional or vocational subjects are useful. During the high tide of specialization this was widely overlooked because people were indoctrinated

to feel that the very concept of usefulness was Philistine—
and because it was relatively easy first to obtain fellowships
and then to land a job. One went wherever one was offered
the most money or prestige and looked down one's nose on
utility.

In the early sixties a graduate student in philosophy who
had not yet completed his doctorate stood a good chance of
being offered a position as an instructor or lecturer with a
salary almost equaling that which the chairman of his department had received at the time of his retirement in the
mid-fifties, just before Sputnik. Those who had a Ph.D. got
more.

This was no time to think about one's goals; for one's
goals did not bear thinking about. Many who felt dimly that
their choices had been dictated by a concern for security and
money, a comfortable and pleasant life in which they were
rather splendidly rewarded for pursuing their own interests,
and that this was perhaps, in one word, selfish, eased their
conscience in the sixties by engaging in rhetoric against the
establishment, middle-class values, and whatever else they
themselves felt guilty of. It was all very understandable
though hardly very thoughtful.

Obviously, something had gone wrong in education some
time before this. When so many people trained in the
humanities, and quite especially in philosophy, had examined their own lives and goals so little, their own training
must have been a far cry from the heritage of Socrates.

Something else had gone wrong, too. Anyone who has
enough imagination keeps thinking of more projects that he
would like to pursue than he has time for. He has to ask
himself: Why should I choose this one above many other
projects? If his central goal is to win academic preferment,
he should be thoughtful and honest enough to admit this to
himself. But it was not only a lack of reflection and candor

that kept people from doing this; it was also a lack of imagination. Most young academics were anything but full of ideas. They had long since gone blind.

A professor's professional life *is* rather pleasant, and apart from having to read examination papers and attend some disheartening committee meetings there are few regular features of it that are more depressing than students explaining that they have to write a thesis and need a topic. One might expect them to come and ask which of many seemed most promising to the professor, but legions cannot think of even one. You cannot expect people in that predicament to give much thought to alternative goals.

There could hardly be a better illustration of scholastic blindness than the fact that in the late sixties and in the early and mid-seventies students kept pouring into graduate programs in the humanities when anyone with eyes to see knew that there were no jobs; and these students were anything but ultra-idealists, fired with enthusiasm for various projects and heedless of security and money. At the same time the graduate schools went right on providing security and some money for three or four years, while refusing to think about the future of their students, once they had their degrees. Blindness had been taught very successfully.

Of course, the students headed for graduate school could plead that no jobs were available for them in any case, or at least no jobs that were as pleasant as another three or four years in school. Everything considered, it was more comfortable to shut one's eyes to the future.

65

Training large numbers of college students in the study of philosophy and religion, literature and music, art and history, requires some justification. Let us consider once more the four major goals of the humanities that I suggested in the prologue.

The first is the conservation and cultivation of the greatest works of the human spirit. I have tried to show how the ways in which the humanities are widely read and taught do not achieve this aim too well. The challenge that artists and writers, philosophers and religious figures, present to us is often, if not usually, ignored. As a rule, the creative human being is ignored altogether, and one concentrates instead on some technical problems posed by one or another work.

Moreover, "elitism" is out of favor, and studies of minor figures and of mass culture are in fashion. Whatever may be said in favor of this trend, it contravenes the first goal of the humanities and also has a dehumanizing effect. In connection with the education of women and blacks much has been said about the importance of role models; and that point is well taken. But we also need models of humanity.

The second goal—that a thoughtful person should reflect on goals, giving attention to alternative visions—has also been a central theme of this book. And the immediate practical results of the refusal to consider aims have been considered, too. Teachers ceased to ask about their obligations to their students and the aims of education. They were no longer interested in the questions why we offer courses on literature or art, religion or philosophy, music or history. They had good reasons for skirting the problem why we should have so many courses in some areas and none in others. For once such questions were asked, the answers were inescapable. The professors were pursuing their own interests. The welfare of the students had dropped out of sight, along with the goals of the humanities.

The one of the four goals that probably fared best, at least in the United States, was the cultivation of a critical spirit. Even here there is no cause for self-congratulation. In some of the best schools, where critical thinking was stressed most, it flourished only within the limits of a rather parochial consensus, because there was insufficient regard for significant alternatives.

One goal remains to be discussed. It is the most problematic of the four: teaching vision.

66

Can vision really be taught? The answer obviously depends on what is meant by vision. As a first answer one might say, the opposite of blindness. Blindness has been taught, and insofar as we can make students less blind and get them to see alternatives as well as their own condition, vision can be taught.

Moreover, it seems useful to distinguish vision of the past, the present, and the future. A teacher of the humanities should open the students' eyes to the past. Much of the work in the humanities must always be historical, though certainly not antiquarian. It is only when we see the past that we gain some perspective on the present. We begin to understand our own condition better, our society, its problems, and contemporary tendencies.

We also gain perspective by obtaining standards of comparison. We realize that what had seemed great often looked that way only because it was so near. Now we can see how it measures up when placed alongside some of the best works of the past. For obvious reasons, many people resist the shattering implications, and in our discussion of reading we have considered some of the ploys they use to maintain their self-importance. They patronize authors whom they might more fittingly read while on their knees. How could they continue to persuade themselves, their administration, and givers of grants that they were revolutionizing their field, working on the frontiers of knowledge, and doing

things of vast significance if they were not blind? To anyone
who has some historical perspective and knows what greatness is, much that is very near seems pitifully small.

Vision of the future cannot be taught. Even the Hebrew
prophets lacked that. Even they could only say, more or
less: Can't you see that if you keep on doing this, such and
such dreadful consequences are all but inevitable? Therefore
stop and change your ways.

Most futurologists claim to be scientific but are deeply
un-Socratic, being loath to admit their ignorance. They
claim to know what they do not know. One of the most
striking facts about the period from 1925 to 1975 is how
those who felt called upon to prophesy made fools of themselves again and again. Who in 1935 or 1945 foresaw the
condition of Germany and Japan in 1965? But people are so
credulous that they quickly forget all the failures and like to
be persuaded by the rare instances when a blind hen finds a
pearl. All errors are forgiven, and the blind hen is called
"prophetic."

It would be idle to try to *forecast* the future of the
humanities, but it makes very good sense to think seriously
about it, asking about the implications of present tendencies
and about the goals that one would like to achieve. Having
done that, one should also ask, as I shall do in the next
chapter, what changes might help to realize these aims. To
think about our future in terms of alternative ends is the
quintessence of responsibility. To eschew consideration of
goals while claiming to predict our future scientifically is
quackery. Some knowledge of the humanities may help one
to grasp the difference.

67

There is yet another sense of vision. Can the kind of vision
that distinguishes the visionary be taught? Is a training in

history, philosophy, religion, art, music, and literature likely to facilitate the development of visionaries? Or is the most that we could hope for more Socratic men and women? One obviously can teach people to think more critically; and any liberal arts college that does not do that is a failure. Any school, on the other hand, that accomplishes this has done humanity some service. Can one also teach originality?

Visionaries, as noted in the chapter on "Four Kinds of Minds," need a mastery of techniques to spell out their vision. They also need discipline to test their hunches and to find out which are worth pursuing. Those who rarely have an idea think that there is something sacrosanct about an intuition, and that the critical and the creative tendencies are incompatible. The truly creative are full of intuitions, hunches, and ideas but have learned to find out, often very quickly, which must be abandoned.

"Progressive" education was persuaded of the value of originality and creativity but failed because it overreacted against the ways in which children were often squelched. "Progressive" educators underestimated the value of discipline and the need for rigorous discrimination among hunches. Children were led to believe that one hunch was as good as another. The age of specialization represented an overreaction against this folly.

The way to facilitate the growth of visionaries is to insist that students go out of their way to look for alternatives and objections. Children could be encouraged even in primary school to think up alternatives—and objections to them. Vision is inseparable from self-criticism, and self-criticism can be constructive. To spell out a vision without any thought of objections to it and without comparison with alternatives is much easier and less impressive, fruitful, and important than an attempt to work out a vision that in a variety of ways seems far superior to rival visions.

It may seem as if that were what science is about. Are the

humanities really needed at this point? They are because a student's work in science is usually more or less microscopic, and the only visions that he is exposed to are those that have stood up under repeated tests. Alternative visions are rarely considered—except in the history of science, which is one of the humanities.

In sum, it is vitally important for humanity in both senses of that word—humane attitudes and mankind—that the humanities should be taught well. Even if they are, there is no guarantee that humanity will survive; but the chances that it will if they are not are almost nil.

CHAPTER SIX:
THE
INTERDISCIPLINARY
AGE

68

By far the best instruction I ever got was in an eight-week course in U.S. Military Intelligence School during World War II. There was no doubt about the purpose of our courses on the battle order of the German army, interpretations of aerial photographs, or interrogation of prisoners. Everything was goal-directed, and there was no time for any nonsense. A captain, who had obtained his rank in the quartermaster corps and who was said to be an expert meat inspector, seemed to be cheating in an examination. Having no hard evidence, the instructor used two different sets of questions in the next test, making sure that each of us got questions different from his neighbors'. When the captain copied his neighbors' answers, he was transferred out of the school. As a captain in military intelligence, he might have done enormous harm.

The men on whom we practiced interrogation were soldiers who had flunked the course. They were properly reluctant to give away the information on which they had been briefed, and surrendered it only under skillful questioning. Given half a chance, they would turn the tables on a blundering interrogator and begin questioning him. It was rough, but nothing easier than that would have made sense.

The roughest part was the Two-Day Test. I took it in January when it was bitterly cold outside. We were taken somewhere at night, by truck, and suddenly were on our own, each alone with a map and a compass. We had to find tent number one, in the dark; and if we missed it by fifty yards, that was that. If you found it, you had no sooner come in out of the cold than you had to take a test and leave again in search of the second tent, where you got the next test. This went on for two days. The idea was that if you knew your stuff only in a cozy room under optimal conditions, you would be a dead loss when your knowledge might be needed.

Our best teacher always walked up and down the center aisle of the classroom during exams, telling jokes. He was exceptionally good at telling them, and it was terribly distracting. He tested us to find out whether we could use what we had learned when there were lots of distractions. There was never any question about the aims of our education, although this lieutenant obviously enjoyed his jokes.

An education in the humanities is not an eight-week crash course, its goals are not the same, and the same methods would not be appropriate. But a good education depends on a clear grasp of goals and the choice of appropriate methods. Too often, discussions about academic requirements, curricula, and the pros and cons of tests and grades make insufficient reference to aims.

I have dealt at length with goals and also with some of the means required to achieve them. Yet something more needs to be said about teaching and the proper mix of specialization and interdisciplinary training.

69

A typical humanities course consists of lectures, reading, and discussion. This makes very good sense. The most important part is reading, to which I have therefore devoted a whole chapter. The lectures and discussions are ancillary, but if they were dispensable there would be no need to have colleges and universities for teaching the humanities. Libraries would be sufficient. But people have to *learn* to read by themselves, and lectures and discussions should be designed to teach them this skill and to make sure that they get ever so much more out of their reading than they would if left to themselves.

Some people consider Oxford tutorials greatly superior to lecture courses—provided one has the luck to get excellent tutors. When a tutor is mediocre or poor, there is no remedy; one is stuck with him for an hour a week, or two hours every other week, and a student cannot shop around as he can for courses. Moreover, a tutor, once elected in his twenties, generally stays on for about forty years; there is very little turnover; and in two years an undergraduate is likely to have three tutors instead of being exposed to many different teachers. The system was designed for the privileged few and is extremely expensive even when tutorials are given to two students at once. It is also extremely cruel to the tutor who has to teach up to eighteen hours a week during three eight-week terms and is almost bound to have some very mediocre students. Under such circumstances a tutor cannot be expected to make the emotional investment required to bring to life a variety of points of view or to probe faith and morals. Nor is it any wonder that he will gratefully admire anyone who provides him with a game he can play with his tutees to make those endless hours bearable. This helps to explain the origins of "Oxford philosophy," which spread to the United States in the fifties.

Wittgenstein had never studied or tutored at Oxford but taught small courses at Cambridge and was deeply involved in his teaching. But at Oxford his approach was adapted in a way that he found utterly repulsive and became a game for tutors—teacups philosophy. His philosophy, which lent itself so easily to this adaptation, was in important ways profoundly un-Socratic from the start. Wittgenstein recoiled from any probe of faith and morals and from social criticism; in his own words, his philosophy leaves everything as it is. A Catholic could remain a Catholic and a Calvinist a Calvinist. This kind of philosophy was easily conformed to the needs of tutors. In any case, the tutorial system has its drawbacks.

Lectures are nevertheless highly problematical, and most of them are certainly a waste of time. If the lecturer does not write them out, chances are that they will be greatly inferior to something available in print that could be assigned instead. And if he does write them out, there seems to be no need for him to read them off because they could easily be made available to the students to read for themselves in half the time. If the professor happens to be exceptionally good at reading his material to an audience, his performance could be put on videotape and made available to students elsewhere, too. If he is bad at it, which is the case more often, the poverty of this whole method of instruction becomes evident.

We must ask whether students would not be better served by very good televised lectures than by mediocre live lectures. Does it make any sense for people who are bad at lecturing to go right on doing it for decades and alienating students? It seems obvious that at the very least something should be done to decrease the percentage of poor lecturers. But in fact there are thousands of colleges and universities in North America alone, the number of professors at many of them is several hundred, and hardly any of them have ever received any advice, not to speak of instruction, about the art with which they earn their living. I doubt that the great majority have ever given very much thought to the point and aims of lecturing. What, if anything, can be achieved in this way that could not be done far better by adding another assignment?

One obvious answer is that a lecture should not go on uninterrupted for the usual fifty minutes, but that lecture and discussion should be combined. But many students become quite impatient with their fellow students who ask questions; they want to hear the professor. That problem can be solved by setting aside periods for discussion in small groups, mostly conducted by younger colleagues or graduate students; by keeping questions during lecture periods short; and if the class is large, by having most of the questions written out and given to the professor before or after the lecture.

That still leaves open the question what the lecturer should try to do when he is not answering questions. Clearly, something that is not done better in some book or article that the students could be asked to read instead. He should exert himself to bring to life the points of view to which the students are exposed, giving of his own blood, soul, and vitality to make the authors speak. The students should read the authors themselves whenever possible; but inconvenient facts, opinions, and arguments are easily over-looked. Every reader tends to see what he likes and not to see what would make him uncomfortable. Least of all does one think of the author as a human being like oneself. The lecturer should try to remedy all that, showing the students how writers not altogether different from themselves could think as they did, and he should lend his own voice to the challenge of the texts.

Authors and texts that do not require any such help need not be used as subjects for lectures but could still be assigned occasionally. There is little excuse for lecturing on what is easily accessible. In the humanities it makes more sense to lecture on what is unfashionable but challenging. On the whole this would work in favor of the greatest authors of past ages. It may be objected that if they are so great and their stature is widely recognized, they are hardly unfashionable. But as they are usually read, and would be read by most students if they were left to themselves, everything in their works that might give offense is overlooked, and their challenge is ignored. Good teachers are needed to expose the students to the vital culture shock.

70

A good teacher has to have vitality. Many undergraduates prize enthusiasm far above scholarship, though they recognize that a fusion of both is even better. When a young teacher with enthusiasm fails to obtain permanent tenure and leaves the faculty, student newspapers often charge that he was "fired" although he was actually one of the best teachers at the whole school. Even during the age of specialization this happened every few years on almost every campus. The first such case I can recall from my own experience occurred in 1940 when I was one of the students who felt that a terrible mistake had been made. Looking back over more than three decades, I find that the batting average of the students in such cases has been very close to zero. It is not difficult to recall teachers who either were not kept on or accepted calls from other schools and subsequently made great reputations elsewhere, but in these cases the students rarely stirred.

It is debatable whether anybody should have permanent

tenure, which confers on professors a degree of security that is not to be found in the business world, for example. The raison d'être of this institution is to guarantee academic freedom. A professor should be free to develop heretical views both in the classroom and in print without fear of being fired. He should be free to probe not only faith and morals and the ideology of his society but also the consensuses in his profession. Having argued that professors ought to do this, I believe that we need permanent tenure to shield them against McCarthyism and against the intolerance of their colleagues. It is depressing that so few professors avail themselves of their privileged position; but I would rather try to influence them to live up to their calling than take away tenure and make the profession even more scholastic.

Now it may be argued whether those who do not obtain tenure after teaching for six years on short-term appointments should not be allowed to stay on without tenure instead of being compelled, as they generally are in the United States, to seek positions elsewhere. As long as it was easy for a good teacher who was denied tenure at one school to obtain it at another, this argument never had much merit. One school's loss was another's gain. Indeed, this was a crucial way for schools that did not require important publications to get teachers who might otherwise have stayed on at the most prestigious universities. In the mid-seventies, when it became desperately difficult for teachers who did not obtain tenure at one school to get a teaching position elsewhere, it became tempting to insist on humanitarian grounds that they ought to be kept on. But keeping them, with tenure or without, would mean that no positions would be left for younger teachers. With funds and the number of positions on the faculty limited, the question is whether one wants to have all positions filled and tell the students that, no matter how bright they may be, they cannot hope to become professors, or whether it is not preferable to have some turnover and competition.

Next, there is the question whether contagious enthusiasm is enough. If the students love a teacher and find him inspiring, it may seem perverse to let him go because he does not publish. But there is a saying that at seventeen the devil's grandmother was pretty. At twenty-seven some of the most boring teachers looked good. It is relatively easy to have some rapport with students and to be full of enthusiasm when one is very young; but those who do no research become stale and often prove to be embarrassing during their last twenty years of teaching. A good school should try to find professors who combine good teaching with good scholarship; and when it lets someone go who was an enthusiastic teacher but not much of a scholar, it can hope to do at least as well in seeking a replacement. Sometimes, of course, it does worse.

The most prestigious schools have often paid far too little attention to the interests of their undergraduates. That is one of the themes of this book. But waiving the emphasis on scholarship and writing would *not* be in the students' interest. It is frightening what professors can get away with in their lectures and in class discussion. What goes over very well in class is not necessarily sound. It is essential for professors to put some of their ideas down on paper and to read them critically the morning after, and a few weeks later. Anyone with a Socratic ethos should occasionally be appalled by his own stuff.

Unfortunately, many people are quite insufficiently self-critical, and it would be an understatement to say that professors are no exception. It is therefore also essential for them to show what they have written to some other scholars to obtain critical appraisals. This eminently sound requirement is often quite unreasonably inflated into the demand that they must publish. The result is that all scholars are in danger of drowning in drivel.

Scholarly journals are full of articles by people who must publish to gain tenure, promotions, or raises in salary. Some deans actually count, and I shall never forget a dean's letter of recommendation for a member of his faculty: "During the past year he has published three times."

Of course, it is not sufficient to show what one has written to a few colleagues who share one's views and are good friends. It is essential to reach out and get reactions from some people whose approach is different and who may question the consensus on which the writer banks. But the present system does not serve this function very well. Far too many things are published that might just as well be circulated in well under fifty copies.

We need to ask of a piece of writing what its purpose might be. If there is some hope that it might stimulate others to look at things in a new light or to pursue new lines of thought and research, then it should be published. If that is not the point, we ought to ask whether the aim could not be reached as well or better by some other method.

In many cases it would make good sense to publish abstracts of papers and then to send Xerox copies of the papers to those who request them. This method would have the additional advantage that, confronted with the need to summarize their contribution in something like five hundred words, many writers might discover for themselves that their papers were not really worth publishing.

71

We need several different kinds of courses and programs to realize the goals defended in this book. I have already described two kinds of courses in the chapter on religion, including one or two broadly conceived courses in comparative religion and an intensive study of the Book of Genesis. What was said there is not difficult to transpose into philosophy and literature, art history and music. But survey courses are profoundly problematical. They were fashionable immediately after World War II, but it was easy to ridicule them, and during the age of specialization they were largely abandoned. To read Dante one week and Shakespeare the next, and then perhaps Spinoza, Milton, Rousseau, Kant, and Goethe, always spending one week on a great book, makes for hopeless superficiality. We certainly should not try to enable students to speak with some semblance of authority about a lot of things they do not know. But offering a one-semester course on each of these great men and nothing that is more comprehensive is bad, too; for in that case most students are bound to graduate without even a basic literacy in the humanities. The function of the comprehensive courses should be clear. The students should be made aware of some of the greatest achievements in each field, and they should be exposed to a variety of points of view and challenges. Whatever specialty they choose, they should have some perspective on it and be able to relate it to some of the best work done in other areas. A whole term's course on a single figure is rarely suitable for undergraduates, much less a whole semester's course on one book. Genesis is an exception, and I have tried to show how a course on that might become the focal point for interdisciplinary explorations that would show the students how religion is related to man's other interests.

It is always easier to be imaginative about courses dealing with a very limited subject matter than about sweeping surveys. Eminently fruitful courses could be devoted to the study of three or four great artists. One might concentrate on painters who lived close to each other in both time and space but who were nevertheless remarkably different. That would give the students some notion of the possibilities of painting and also expose them to some striking and challenging alternatives. They would explore some very different ways of looking at the world.

Bosch influenced Pieter Bruegel the Elder, but both are

among the most original artists of all time. Rubens owned a
dozen of Bruegel's paintings, but he represents a third sensibility. And Rembrandt, who was Rubens' younger contemporary, offers us yet another world. A course on these
four painters could be unforgettable.

This formula could obviously be varied. Another course
could be built around Grünewald, Dürer, Michelangelo, and
Titian, for example.

No two-term sequence could possibly cover the history of
art without becoming superficial. Nevertheless, such a sequence is badly needed to open the students' eyes to the
world's art and to provide them with some framework and
perspective into which they could then hope to fit their own
explorations—further   courses,   art   books,   visits   to
museums, and trips to other parts of the world. Concentrat-
ing on sculpture and painting, one might devote two weeks
each during the first semester to Egypt, to Mesopotamia and
Iran, to Greece, to India, and to China and Japan. The
second term one might spend two weeks each on Europe
before 1400; the Italian Renaissance; the Low Countries,
Germany, France, and Spain; modern art from Manet
through Picasso; and pre-Columbian and "primitive" art.
This sounds rather barbarous, and yet it would serve undergraduates better than having most of them graduate without
the slightest knowledge of the world of the visual arts.

In literature, too, it is easy to think of good courses dealing with four major figures. Homer, Aeschylus, Sophocles,
and Euripides belonged to the same culture and tradition and
could be studied in some depth even in ten weeks. One
would not have to start all over again every time to get some
sense of the context. Having read Homer and Aeschylus,
one has some knowledge of the background of Sophocles
and Euripides. The disadvantage of this procedure is that
one is likely to end up with alternatives that are too similar
to each other, unless one guards against this. The four poets

mentioned, like the artists mentioned earlier, are exceptional in embodying different outlooks with singular power.

Still, the spread could be increased by including writers from different cultures. To avoid superficiality, one might choose two from each of two languages. Goethe, Tolstoy, Dostoevsky, and Kafka could be the subject of a fascinating course. It should include *Faust, Anna Karenina* and *Resurrection, Crime and Punishment* and *The Brothers Karamazov,* and *The Trial* and *The Castle,* along with some shorter supplementary pieces by each of the four authors. They worked in a single European tradition and dealt with similar themes, allowing the teacher to avoid the shallowness that earned survey courses such a bad repute. Yet the four represent very different attitudes.

What is much harder is to think of broad courses that would acquaint the students with a good deal of material without becoming shallow. At the very least, we should have one-term courses on the history of French, English, German, and Russian literature, to give only four examples.

The point of these illustrations is merely to flesh out the implications of the preceding chapters. Too often course offerings reflect the research interests of a department that is not very broad in its sympathies. College catalogues are often misleading by listing many courses that are hardly ever given. We should give more thought to the education undergraduates receive.

72

Philosophy needs a little more space here than do art and literature, though not nearly as much as religion, to which I have devoted a whole chapter. At Oxford, philosophy has long been central in humanistic education, and if one believes in the importance of Socrates' ethos one must concede to philosophy a special place. Philosophy as taught at

Oxford and at many American colleges and universities since World War II, on the other hand, certainly does not merit any central place in humanistic education. As I see it, courses in religion, art, and literature can accomplish a great deal of what needs to be done. Certainly, the necessary culture shock can be experienced in these studies. But when we confront these challenges and try to sort out our thoughts, we get into philosophy.

Here we need at least three different kinds of courses. Once again, it is not too difficult to organize a few courses around some major figures. Plato is *sui generis;* he is the one philosopher who should be studied for a whole term. Indeed, there could hardly be a better introduction to philosophy than a course on him in which the students read the *Symposium, Apology,* and *Crito,* the last pages of the *Phaedo* that describe the death of Socrates, and the *Republic*. The image of Socrates will haunt many students through the rest of their days, challenging them to examine their lives and reflect on their goals; and Plato's sustained and very controversial discussion of ends in the *Republic* can easily be taught in such a way that it provides a profound culture shock.

These readings were quite popular at one time, although the *Symposium* was not usually included. But in teaching the *Republic* many professors followed the example of F. M. Cornford, whose English version with commentary is admirable in many other ways but seeks to eliminate any offense the book might give. Thus Cornford suggested quite implausibly that Plato's withering attack on democracy was applicable only to Athenian democracy. Had Plato only known how wonderfully democracy works in our time!

During the fifties I taught such a course for some time, using Cornford like my predecessor. He had followed Cornford's line, I didn't, and the course always went over very well both ways. If I were to give it again, I would expand the reading list and include also at the very least Pericles' funeral oration about Athenian democracy, as reported by Thucydides, and—by way of expanding the discussion of civil disobedience in connection with the *Apology* and *Crito*—Sophocles' *Antigone*. Plato as well as his original readers must have known both, and the students would understand him better if they did, too. Also, they would confront some memorable alternatives.

Another way of exposing students to a powerful challenge is to have them read Nietzsche. His impact is not softened by the filter of a Plato, and the medicine of a whole term of Nietzsche might well be too strong for many students. It seems better to divide such a course between Nietzsche and two, or at most three, other writers. For many years I have taught an upper-class course called "Hegel, Nietzsche, and Existentialism." In recent years, half of the reading has usually been in Nietzsche, with the other half divided between Hegel, Kierkegaard, and Sartre. The aim was always to catch the students in the cross fire of radically divergent points of view. It is arguable that the inclusion of Hegel is too much, and that the other three would be sufficient. At the time I shaped the course, nobody else at Princeton had any interest in teaching Hegel, while I found him exceptionally interesting. But the idea was never to make the students feel in the end that now they knew Hegel, but only to expose them to a very striking alternative that at the same time helps us understand many later writers, including Kierkegaard and Sartre.

The two broad courses in philosophy have already been referred to in Chapter 1, "Four Kinds of Minds." Philosophy majors as well as students in other departments who want to take a little philosophy ought to be offered a two-term sequence in the history of philosophy. This was common practice in American colleges before the age of specialization—and ought to be restored with some modifications. The common American notion of the history of philosophy was rather academic; it was really the history of the theory of knowledge and excluded ethics and political philosophy, not to speak of philosophy of art or of religion. Nor was it usual to confront the students with powerful alternatives. Either one offered them a smorgasbord, *ganz unverbindlich,* without any obligation on their part, or more rarely one followed Hegel's lead and traced a historical development that represented progress in some sense.

To spread out the sequence over more than two terms is counterproductive because in that case few students will take the whole of it. The advantage of two terms is that many will, and philosophy majors can and should be required to take it. But it poses a difficult problem of selection. It seems best to stick with the old practice of devoting one term to the Greeks and the second to the period from Descartes to Kant.

Ancient philosophy would begin with the pre-Socratics, devoting two or three weeks to them, and stressing Heraclitus, Parmenides and Zeno, and Democritus, including his ethic as well as his atomism. Then I would study Plato for at least three weeks, avoiding any extensive overlap with the Plato course. One might concentrate on the *Meno,* either *Protagoras* or *Gorgias, Phaedrus, Timaeus,* and parts of *The Laws.* Aristotle might be represented by parts of his *Physics, Metaphysics,* and *Nicomachean Ethics,* as well as a few shorter selections. After three weeks of Aristotle, the students could still get some idea of Stoicism, Epicureanism, and ancient skepticism. One could hardly avoid tracing developments; but I would insist on confronting the student nevertheless with a series of striking alternatives.

In the modern philosophy course it would be a shame to have to omit any of the following eight philosophers: Descartes, Hobbes, Spinoza, Locke, Leibniz, Berkeley,

Hume, and Kant. In a twelve-week course, half of them could be studied for two weeks each; say, Descartes, Spinoza, Hume, and Kant. In a ten-week term only two of the eight could be studied for more than one week, and one would certainly need at least two weeks for Kant.

The British empirical tradition is not likely to provide much of a culture shock for English-speaking students. It is nevertheless vitally important. One way of dealing with it in the spirit of the other suggestions made here would be to devote a course to Kant and either Hume or John Stuart Mill. Kant could then be studied for at least six weeks, and either Hume or Mill for at least four. In each case it would be highly desirable to give the students some idea of the man's whole philosophy and outlook, not only of his theory of knowledge. One could read Hume's short autobiography and his two great "Enquiries" as well as his *Dialogues concerning Natural Religion*. In the case of Kant the obvious assignments would be parts of the *Critique of Pure Reason* and the whole of the *Foundation of the Metaphysics of Morals*. It would be worthwhile to add parts of his *Religion within the Bounds of Mere Reason Alone* and the whole of his brilliant *Idea for a Universal History with Cosmopolitan Intent,* the short essay in which Kant proposed a League of Nations after developing a philosophy of history that profoundly influenced Hegel and Marx. In the lectures the students could be given some idea of the works not studied in the course. This would also apply to Mill, whose *Utilitarianism* and *On Liberty* would be obvious choices to which one might add one or two of his other major works.

Students who already know a book well should always be encouraged to read an alternative assignment, it being understood that having read a great book *once* does not mean that one knows it well. The central aim of all those courses would never be to make the students feel that now they know what there is to be known about the subject. It would always be to lead them to examine their own faith and morals and assumptions, as well as the consensuses by which they are surrounded. That is not to say that knowledge would be played down. The students should be shown how they need knowledge and how their reading is relevant to some questions that merit attention.

Philosophy, of course, is not just history of philosophy. The usual fare includes many systematic courses. My paradigmatic suggestion about social philosophy, in section 9 of the first chapter, applies equally to ethics and philosophy of religion, to theory of knowledge and aesthetics. The students ought to be exposed to writers who have argued with some skill and power for alternative positions.

It stands to reason that within a few years, if not months, most of the students will forget most of the details. Professors should ask themselves what, if anything, they would like to leave with their students for the rest of their lives. If a friend can teach you in a few minutes to stand on your head, and after that you think of him every time you do it, it should be possible to teach at least some students something in the course of a whole term that they will be happy not to forget.

Professors who are doing research usually try hard to keep up with the latest articles on their subject, and in recent years many collections of articles have been published in topical paperbacks. But most such literature is quickly dated, if not quite as fast as weekly magazines. On the whole, undergraduates are ill served by assignments of this sort. Even books about which everybody in the profession got excited when they first appeared are often felt to be quite poor a few years later. This is no reason for not also having students read something contemporary, but in the humanities one should not lightly slight material that has worn well for a century or more. Of course, I am far from suggesting that students should be urged to *accept* ideas merely because they are old.

73

Interdisciplinary work is often relegated to the first two years of college, it being understood that one must specialize as one grows up. Obviously, such work cannot be serious as long as those who do it have not yet mastered at least two disciplines. Thus this system provides easy confirmation for its false assumption that interdisciplinary work is not serious.

Nevertheless, a teacher who brings to his lectures for nineteen-year-old students perspectives he has gained through work in different disciplines may well offer an exceptionally valuable and exciting course. If he has the competence to guide his students through materials in different disciplines, he may open their eyes to unforeseen connections and meanings. Chapters 2 and 4, "The Art of Reading" and "The Place of Religion in Higher Education," provide various illustrations.

To understand the meaning and significance of a text it is frequently imperative for the reader to do some interdisciplinary work. The reluctance to take this step is often due not only to the misgivings that one might lack sufficient competence but also to the fear of culture shock. The blinders provided by specialization can often save us from this unsettling experience.

Every text has a context. The context of great plays or novels is not purely literary; the context of a philosophical classic is not exclusively philosophical; the context of a religious scripture is not only religious; and the context of the paintings on the ceiling of the Sistine Chapel is not made up solely of other paintings. It would be misleading to say that the humanities interpenetrate. It would be more to the point to realize that any attempt to divide them up into departments is bound to result in artificial borderlines. A departmental approach is always abstract; it refuses to look at a concrete whole in its exceedingly complex context and concentrates instead on one facet of a work, or perhaps on a few aspects. This is not necessarily bad. It is often immensely interesting to look at something through a microscope, and in this way one may discover beauties that had escaped the naked eye. But one should not forget that one is looking through a microscope. One should not mistake a tiny piece of tissue for the elephant from whose tail it was removed without his ever noticing.

Even many small details are often misinterpreted because the reader or the viewer overlooks the immediate context— say, of a sentence on a page or in a chapter. Scholasticism always tends toward a disregard for context and is to that extent opposed to humanism and the ethos of the humanities. In German, the nearest equivalent to "humanities" is *Geisteswissenschaften,* which means spiritual sciences as opposed to the natural sciences. (The nearest English equivalent to that, in turn, is mental sciences, a term that was still in use less than a hundred years ago.) Goethe's Mephistopheles lampooned the scholastic mind even in the *Urfaust,* written in the early 1770s, saying that the analysts always begin by driving out the spirit (*Geist*), and that in the end they hold the parts in their hand, minus the spirit that held them together. *A fortiori,* this kind of mind ignores the larger context that requires interdisciplinary study.

The scholastic may reply that progress depends on abstraction, which is true. One must be able to focus on some details, on certain main lines, or on aspects that are relevant to some particular problem, while excluding a hundred irrelevancies that do not matter for the moment. But it is equally true that progress depends on the discovery of connections between things that had not been seen together before. It may be a crucial connection between details that had been thought to belong to different disciplines; it may also be an interesting relationship between somewhat larger units that cannot be seen at all as long as one looks through a microscope. Often one has to stand back or even view something from a considerable distance before one notices what, once seen, seems so obvious that it is hard to understand how anyone could have failed to be struck by it.

These considerations explain why outsiders have often played important parts in various disciplines. But the moral is not that the pure fool is far superior to the specialists, and that students should be educated to become pure fools. After all, the percentage of fools, pure or not, who make discoveries of some importance is minute; and so is the percentage of those who are outsiders in relation not only to one science but to all. The moral is that we need more interdisciplinary work. People with disciplined minds who know what research is and how one tests a hunch, having learned all this in one or two disciplines, are quite likely to bring a new and interesting perspective to another discipline, perceiving problems, similarities, connections, and absurdities that specialists in this field had overlooked. Whenever that happens, the scholastic specialists suddenly look like a lot of blind moles who build their structures in the dark and feel happy when they find an insect.

We cannot turn moles into eagles; but opening people's eyes is what education is all about. Vision can be taught to some extent, and one of the important ways of doing that is to show students the need for interdisciplinary work.

This can be shown at all levels, but one should also insist at all levels that serious interdisciplinary work requires discipline and competence in at the very least two fields or departments. To this end, the students need role models as well as examples of the contributions made possible by such training. Examples are not hard to find. The interdisciplinary prowess of the major philosophers of the past meets the eye, but scholastic professors have generally ignored such inconvenient facts. Those interested in mathematics may have stressed Descartes's and Leibniz's mathematical genius; but few have ever thought of asking whether a thinker's most characteristic ideas might have something to do with his work in other fields.

The most interesting contributions to the study of religion, literature, and art have always been made by people with a base in several fields, while hyperspecialists were reduced to playing games assigning verses in Genesis to J_1, E_2, or P_3, or tracing tropes in long poems. An art historian who did not know much about literature, religion, and general history would be a joke. Surely, the same is true of experts in at least some of the other humanities.

74

Again the image of concentric circles may prove helpful. The innermost circle represents an academic department, the next circle the whole of the humanities. Man is one, and in a way the humanities are one, and the humanist must constantly cross departmental frontiers.

The third circle contains all of the arts and sciences, including the social and natural sciences. It would be wonderful if one could be at home in all of them, but with the expanse of knowledge since the early nineteenth century that is no longer possible. Nor would it be fruitful to try to go as far as possible along this road, as one would die while still a graduate student. The way to do something worthwhile is to work on some specific projects and problems and then to see what kind of competence is needed to get on with them. It may be psychology or economics, or both, biology, physics, or mathematics. Often one has to turn for help to friends in other fields, at the very least to check one's findings. This is scarcely news for philosophers. Even during the age of specialization, respect for the sciences led many of them to look now and then into one or another science, if only a social one. They actually did this more often than they looked into the other humanities.

Even these three circles are insufficient. Work on some of the most serious problems that confront humanity all but compels us to reach out still further. Nor should we hide this fact from our students. An education in the humanities should involve professional schools, too, notably including law and medicine. Two examples may show how even this is not enough. There is a fifth circle that includes not only arts and sciences and professional schools but also the rest of human life.

75

Punishment has often been discussed in philosophy courses, in religion courses, in courses on Greek tragedy taught in the department of classics, in courses on Russian novels, in political theory, psychology, sociology, and anthropology, as well as law schools. We should build a whole semester's work around problems of punishment.

The students would read relevant literature in all the fields mentioned and listen to professors from different disciplines. The point would not be to try to find out all the foolish things that have been said about punishment but only to sample some of the follies and to gain some sense of the limitations of every departmentalized approach; to see how such approaches complement one another and how, if at all, they illuminate problems of vast importance to live human beings. To that end, the students would also attend some trials, and they would be required to do some practical work, preferably some teaching, in prisons, under circumstances that would allow them to listen to the prisoners and to learn as well as teach.

It is a disgrace that, in countries that are proud of their well-informed citizenry and are built on ballots and the jury system, one can get all sorts of degrees and be certified not only as an educated person but even as a teacher without ever having followed a trial or been inside a prison. One can even become a judge and sentence people to prison without ever having spent one night in a prison. We ought to know how our society punishes people, and we should consider the pros and cons of our system and of some alternatives.

The humanities would profit from this suggestion not only because humanists and students headed for humanities would learn a great deal in this way but also because it would allow humanists to contribute something worthwhile to the education of lawyers, judges, social workers, and colleagues in the social sciences. The point would not be to gain more students for existing courses in nine or ten departments; there would not be time to take that many courses in one term, in addition to attending trials and teaching in prison. A special integrated program would be designed for this purpose, with readings, lectures, and discussions in all the areas mentioned above, and supplemented with an exhibition of appropriate works of art, showings of relevant films, and performances of suitable plays. For one term the students would live with the problems of punishment.

It would be difficult in academic life to kill more birds with one stone. Future judges and lawyers as well as students in the social sciences and the humanities would find a semester like that one of their most valuable educational experiences. It would also go far to satisfy the legitimate desire for relevance and the impatience that precisely many of the best and most sensitive students feel in the face of their isolation from real life. Nor should the following point be overlooked. By beginning with real life problems, we quickly discover the limits of our traditional departmentalization and of scholasticism. We come to see the need for interdisciplinary studies and Socratic questioning. Finally,

such a reexamination of conventional attitudes and procedures could hardly fail to influence our attitudes and our
behavior toward those who are punished, including not only
convicts but also children.

76

Dying is another subject on which philosophers have
written—usually rather badly—and it is also discussed in
religion and literature courses, in psychology, sociology,
and anthropology, and in medical schools. We should build
another whole semester's work around problems of aging
and dying.

The case closely parallels that of punishment. Future
nurses and doctors could profit from exposure to relevant
material in the arts and sciences, while students of arts and
sciences would be brought to realize the limitations of traditional departmentalized approaches. Again, there could
also be an art exhibit, and the students would see relevant
films and plays. They would listen to gerontologists and
physicians, and they would be required to do some practical
work in nursing homes and hospitals.

Most of the major German poets from Klopstock and
Goethe to Rilke and Gottfried Benn have written fascinating
poems about death. A study of these poems throws far more
light on human attitudes toward death than do Heidegger's
turgid and dogmatic pronouncements about "Being-
toward-Death" in his *Being and Time* (1927). This may
sound dogmatic, too, but those who wonder whether this is
true will find more than a score of such poems in my
Twenty-Five German Poets: A Bilingual Collection (1975),
and in the last three chapters of *Existentialism, Religion,
and Death* (1976) I argue this case. In a course one might
ask whether this selection of poems is representative of
German poetry; what additional illumination might be

gained from the drama or the novel; whether we find different attitudes in English, French, or Greek literature; and how attitudes toward death are influenced by historical conditions, by religion, by youth or age, by tuberculosis, cancer, or war. One might compare poets dying of consumption, like Novalis, Schiller, and Keats; and one might juxtapose Benn's "Man and Woman Walk Through the Cancer Ward" with Rilke's last poem, written a few days before he died of leukemia. If most students think of poetry as quite remote from real life and in some sense irrelevant, this is surely due in large measure to the ways in which poetry has been taught for the most part. The quality of most poetry that is politically committed does not help. Students need to be shown how outstanding poets and artists have dealt with problems with which philosophers and social scientists, lawyers and physicians, try to deal, too.

Many people think of the visual arts as at most illustrative. Käthe Kollwitz (1867–1945), surely the greatest woman artist of all time, might teach them how wrong that is. She etched her first *Death* when she was still in her twenties; and the first of her five cycles, *Weavers' Rebellion,* done the year she turned thirty, includes another *Death.* Few artists, if any, have ever explored this theme so thoroughly. Early drawings and etchings, done before 1914, show a mother with a dead child, a woman going into the water to drown herself, *Run Over,* and Death taking a woman from her child. After 1914 she returned often to these themes and also did many widows, including some surrounded by their terrified children. In *Death Reaches for a Woman,* the woman clutches her infant and seems dominated by the thought: What is to become of the child? But around the same time (1923/24) Kollwitz also portrayed Death as a woman comforting a woman.

Except for a few sculptures, Kollwitz concentrated on the graphic arts, dealing all her life long with the sufferings wrought by war and extreme poverty. Color she shunned as if it were a diversion, and her portrayals of grief and despair remain unexcelled. In 1924 she drew herself as *Seated Woman with the Hand of Death,* leaving no doubt that her own death held no terror for her. Another charcoal drawing, ten years later, bears the title *Woman Welcomes Death.*

Her last cycle, a series of eight lithographs (1934) called "Death," includes *Death Recognized as a Friend* and *The Call of Death*—a beautiful self-portrait, once again with the hand of Death. Like her last self-portrait, which shows her in profile, a little stooped, looking old, it expresses a deeply moving readiness to die.

It is shocking that one can get a higher education and degrees in the humanities without ever facing up to the problems of dying. One can get away with discussing philosophical and literary treatments of the subject while refusing to look at the facts, though in this case none of us can say that they do not concern us and the people closest to us. It is doubtful whether the humanities can have much of a future if they shirk the greatest contributions they can make. In conjunction with other disciplines, they can and should help us to gain a better understanding of such serious problems as punishment and dying and make us more humane.

The list of problems could easily be lengthened. The whole growing field of bioethics is a case in point. It has come into focus only recently, but virtually everyone who thinks about it seems to be agreed on the need for interdisciplinary cooperation. In this spirit the editors of a new *Encyclopedia of Bioethics* have asked scholars in a large number of different fields to contribute articles. Clearly, nothing else would do, and the problems of abortion, euthanasia, suffering, cloning, and experiments on animals and people do require some intelligent, informed discussion. Yet the academic world is still heavily weighted in favor of narrow specialization.

As matters now stand, it has been said that in a modern urban hospital the only generalist is the patient. In the modern university the only generalist is the undergraduate. This has to be changed, and the humanities will have to play a central role in the change.

77

Cynics may say that scholasticism has a stranglehold on "the establishment," that highly specialized studies are still what is supported by grants, published by professional journals, and rewarded by raises and promotions, and that nothing can be done about that. But I wonder. It has been said that nothing in the world can stop an idea whose time has come. That is either overly optimistic or, more likely, a hollow tautology. If the idea is stopped, it follows that its time had not yet come; and perhaps it never will. But it is unworthy of a humanist to bank on the wave of the future.

When we have given a matter a great deal of thought and reached the conclusion that the current state of affairs is bad and that something should be done about it, it is contemptible if we hold our peace merely because we cannot be sure of success. Anyone who has that little faith in the power of ideas should not be a writer and a teacher.

Having attempted a diagnosis and prescription, I still need to ask how we can provide incentives for people to take the prescription. How can we move education in a new direction?

That students would flock to the programs outlined here, we need not doubt. Nor need we doubt that scholastics, losing students, would insinuate that what is popular is usually not rigorous and cannot be respectable. I share in the suspicion of all that is popular, but I extend it to what is popular with scholastics. Traveling in schools, they are for the most part creatures of fashion who are all too much concerned with the direction of the wind. Their contempt for popularity does not extend beyond courses, books, and people that they do not like in the first place. Many of them have assigned Camus and other fashionable authors and introduced topics like abortion into their courses when *they* became fashionable, hoping to attract students. Many changed their hair styles, clothing, and opinions to conform to fashions set by students. It has been suggested that they did this to remain young. What is the difference? They wanted to ''be with it.'' They accepted the fashionable values of youth and popularity. And if the wind changed its direction and popularity required it, they would eagerly join, but try to make everything as scholastic as possible.

As long as all the big rewards are given to scholastic specialists, most graduate students, younger scholars and older scholars as well, will continue to do what pays, choosing popularity with those in power even above popularity with students. It is not difficult to say what those in power ought to do to change the whole scene. In brief, they should provide incentives for people to do what badly needs to be done. All that is necessary is, as Plato noted long ago, that the kings should become philosophers or the philosophers kings. But if the salt has lost its savor, and the philosophers have become scholastics, the situation may seem hopeless. For university administrations, foundations, and grants committees always must rely on expert advice, and the ranking experts in every field are usually scholastics.

For a number of reasons, however, there is hope. I shall mention only three, in ascending order of importance. The first alone would carry little weight.

The humanities are in rather obvious trouble, and self-doubt is pervading the profession. One senses that something has gone wrong without being sure what, and hence one is not totally unreceptive to a diagnosis and prescription.

Second, the importance of interdisciplinary work is coming to be recognized more and more widely. Conferences that involve scholars from many different fields are "in," and symposia of this type are being published. There are several new interdisciplinary journals, and the establishment of new interdisciplinary centers is under way. Nor can all this be shrugged off as unscientific. The need for interdisciplinary approaches is widely recognized by scientists, and the microscopists in the humanities will soon realize with a shock that they are behind the times. Holism used to bring to mind General Jan Smuts and his philosophy. It was considered "soft." Systems used to be associated with Hegelian philosophers. Now holistic "systems" approaches are "in." The interdisciplinary age has begun.

Finally, the crisis that overtook higher education in much of the world in the early seventies demands drastic changes. There no longer are jobs for young Ph.D.'s. Thousands who received their doctorates since the late sixties have not found teaching positions, and the outlook for those who have entered graduate schools since then is dismal. It is an extraordinary example of scholastic blindness that during this period most graduate schools have gone right on admitting as many students as before and turning out Ph.D.'s. Most graduate programs in the humanities will have to be curtailed drastically in the very near future. At that point, professors will have to give more attention to their undergraduates, and they may even become receptive to the view that the main thrust of undergraduate education should not be to duplicate at a lower level what is done in graduate school. This does not mean that the wave of the future is about to sweep in the reforms proposed in this book. But it does mean that right now it would be the height of irresponsibility not to give serious thought to the future of the humanities.

Specifically, the time has come to plan seriously for interdisciplinary centers that, for logistical reasons, will have to be associated with universities. Such centers should provide incentives for professors who want to do interdisciplinary work of a high order. They should provide reduced teaching for those planning new courses, and an environment in which those engaged in such work could easily talk and compare notes with others who are also engaged in interdisciplinary work. Fellows would be invited from other universities and from the professions, including law and medicine as well as business and politics. They would be asked to give public lectures that would make those outside these centers aware of the centers; and they would also participate in interdisciplinary seminars to which their expertise could contribute something. The centers would help to break down the barriers between professors and people in the outside world from whom they could learn something, and they would make it easy for people not employed by a university to return now and then to a university environment and profit from that. The centers would host *small* conferences at which people from different backgrounds would discuss intensively for a few days problems of mutual interest. Such programs as those concerned with punishment and dying could be sponsored by such centers.

Finally, we need some new journals. One shudders to say this when there are far too many journals even now, and nobody can keep up any more with the flood of articles. But as we have seen, a whole dimension of discourse has been lost. Where can nonprofessors and professors talk to each other in print about subjects of vital mutual concern? Where could, say, the chapter on ''Four Kinds of Minds'' or ''The Art of Reading'' have been published—and reached the audience for which it is intended? There is no forum for discussions of this kind. The interdisciplinary journals we have do not fill the very real need of which I speak here.

Strong-minded individuals will follow their own lights

anyway, but our education has bred conformity, and we should look for ways in which the kind of writing and teaching we need is rewarded. Interdisciplinary centers could help us to do this.

This book is not a blueprint for a new academy. It is a call for serious reflection. The question is not what will happen, but rather: What do we wish to happen? What kind of future would we like to build?

ACKNOWLEDGMENTS

The Rockefeller Foundation very graciously invited me to write this book at the Villa Serbelloni, to which I have paid tribute in an earlier book, *Without Guilt and Justice*. The Foundation and the resident directors, William and Betsy Olson, provided ideal working conditions, including a small study in the woods, on the edge of a high cliff, in a setting that brings to mind a great Chinese painting in which one has to search for the scholar's abode. This made it easier to gain the distance needed to discuss such a large subject.

During the two months preceding my stay at the Villa I was a Visiting (Research) Professor in the Institute of Philosophy at the Hebrew University in Jerusalem while I was the guest of Mishkenot Shaananim and had every reason to feel that I was living in the heavenly Jerusalem. I am profoundly grateful to the international selection committee and to Teddy Kollek, the mayor of Jerusalem, for inviting me. This was one of the best things that has ever happened to me. It was here that I wrote the first draft of the first chapter, which I then presented both at the Van Leer Jerusalem Foundation and at Tel Aviv University. The discussion after the lectures proved helpful. I owe special thanks to Yehuda Elkana for his detailed comments.

It was also in Jerusalem that I was asked by an Israeli how one could best teach the Bible to young men and women who have no religious faith nor any knowledge of religion. I tried to answer him, and he urged me to write about this problem. Being made in Jerusalem, this request haunted me. It helped to give shape to Chapter 4.

In the fall of 1974, before I went to Jerusalem, I was a Visiting Fellow in the History of Ideas Unit in the Research School of Social Sciences at the Australian National University. My main project was in the history of ideas, but in November I presented to the philosophers at the Research School some of the ideas that eventually went into Chapter 2. In March I tried them out again at the Hebrew University, still using a brief outline, and Gershom Scholem's opposition led me to write up my ideas in a slightly different form and, of course, in greater detail, as soon as I arrived at the Villa Serbelloni; and then there was no stopping until I had finished the whole book and revised the draft of the first chapter, too. At that point Douglas Verney, also a visiting scholar at the Villa, had the great kindness to read the whole draft and discuss it with me, while I went on with the work of revision.

To Princeton University I owe the leave of absence that made it possible for me to go to Australia, Jerusalem, and Bellagio. This leave was made doubly beautiful by the companionship of my wife, Hazel.

When I consider all the generosity showered on me during these past months, I feel that it may require some explanation why the book is not mellower. In the midst of so much beauty, written in a study with stunning views of the Lago di Como, how could these pages fail to be suffused with gratitude? It is impossible not to enjoy this setting, but that does not make the state of the humanities rosier.

I know no other place where I could have finished a complete draft of this book in something like five weeks, nor any other place where the temptation to take a kindly view of everything was greater. Having found out long ago how nasty academics often are in conversation and how mild they are in print, I adopted this

Motto

Never write pap
and be bitchy in speech.
Be gentle as Moses
and write with wrath.

Lackeys are mellowed
by recognition.
Moses was not
by the friendship of God.

I have never been honored with any remotely comparable friendship and certainly do not see myself as another Moses. I merely leaned over backwards not to be gentle in print.

After returning to Princeton in May, I revised my manuscript very extensively in the light of second thoughts and also profited from the reactions of others, most notably my friend Siegwart Lindenberg, a superb critic who gave me a very hard time, as usual. When I had rewritten the manuscript and got it accepted for publication, Alvin Kernan, Dean of the Graduate School at Princeton, and Adam Morton read it and made further suggestions. When I had taken these into account, Professor Morton looked at the revisions once more. It is one of the greatest blessings of the academic world that it provides a setting in which many friendships of this kind flourish.

Index